Being a Parent

University of Toronto Press

Karl S. Bernhardt

Being a Parent

Unchanging Values in
a Changing World

edited by
David K. Bernhardt

© University of Toronto Press 1970

Reprinted in paperback 2014

ISBN 978-0-8020-1645-4 (cloth)

ISBN 978-0-8020-6106-5 (paper)

To two pioneers of Child Study in Canada

Contents

Foreword

Being a parent in the seventies is a challenging responsibility. It has been in any era. However the world and life patterns have been changing so rapidly that parents are confused about their role and their duties, and even question their own significance.

Karl Bernhardt has much to say to parents of the seventies: though times have changed, the fundamental values of human relationships have not. These still form the roots of personality growth. Children still need parents, for it is through these close early relationships that the beginnings of humanness are established; they still need guidelines for patterns of action and indeed forms of restraint (this is what used to be called discipline!) and they still need support and encouragement as they grow away from the shelter of the family to become men and women in their own right.

Karl Bernhardt had great faith in parents and as a psychologist he was fully aware that it is the family that is the basic influence in personality development. Institutions, such as education, are important but supplementary to the family unit. It is not surprising therefore that those who knew Karl best say that of his many interests – psychology, nursery education, administration, teaching – parent education was central throughout the years. This book reflects and expands what he wrote in the *Parent Education Bulletin* in 1939:

> Parent education is not a cult, a religion, or a fashion. Rather it is an attempt on the part of serious-minded people to bring our stock of knowledge about human nature and relationships to bear on the business of living together in the family and on the training of children for responsible citizenship. There is much that we still need to know about family life and child training. So, parent education must continue a brisk interest in research. On the other hand there is a great deal of available information about human behavior which can be applied with profit. This application must be made by the individual and not merely by experts. Our main method in parent education is not telling parents what to do but rather helping them to think out their own solutions and methods.

So too, the main purpose of this book is not to tell parents what to do in the 1970s, but rather to help them think out their own solutions and methods in the light of basic and unchanging values.

It has been a privilege for the W. E. Blatz Memorial to encourage and support the publication of this book. For Karl Bernhardt was a student, colleague, and friend of Dr. Blatz and for over thirty years worked and taught at the Institute of Child Study, University of Toronto. As assistant director under Dr. Blatz his main responsibility was the development of a parent education programme. As part of this he edited the *Bulletin* from 1938 to 1964. He was its first and only permanent editor. On Dr. Blatz's retirement in 1960 Karl Bernhardt became the Institute's second director and remained in this position until his retirement in 1964.

It is also appropriate that David Bernhardt should have compiled his father's papers and seen them through to publication. David and his father began the editing together; David completed the task on his own. A product has resulted with which, I am sure, Karl Bernhardt would have been very pleased.

The Blatz Memorial is grateful to have been associated with this project. It hopes that Karl's wisdom and knowledge will make Being a Parent in the seventies not merely a challenging, but an exhilarating experience.

MARY L. NORTHWAY
for the W. E. Blatz Memorial Committees
The Brora Centre, Toronto, Canada

Preface

Over thirty years Karl Bernhardt wrote hundreds of articles and gave hundreds of talks for parents on the best way to bring up children. Many of these articles have been brought together here. Each of the articles was originally written as a separate address to parents on a specific topic. Therefore they may be consulted individually as suggestions on specific topics.

There is a common philosophy, however, which can be seen throughout all the articles. It is a philosophy which Karl Bernhardt lived. It is a philosophy which has its roots in a belief in the worth of each individual and what that individual says, feels, and thinks no matter how young he may be.

Associated with this belief in the worth of the individual (and especially those who are young and growing) are the goals of developing a feeling of security in the individual and a method of discipline which is consistent, immediate, invariable, and logical. Many parents find it difficult to follow this approach to child rearing while at the same time admitting its common sense nature. To be completely successful it must become part of the personality of the individuals involved and this is something that does not happen over night. It is as much a way of life as a bag of tricks. I hope some of the spirit of that way of life comes through these articles which represent a life time of effort at explaining this total philosophy of family relationships.

Over the years Karl Bernhardt wrote more than two hundred articles (a bibliography of these appears at the end of this book). Some of them are revisions of earlier articles and some had nothing to do with the theme of this book. In putting together the articles for this book the editor's first job, therefore, was to select the most appropriate and the most recent. Once selected and grouped into chapters they were edited to remove as much of the repetition as possible and in some cases rewritten to bring them up to date and include more recent references.

DAVID K. BERNHARDT
Carleton University
Ottawa, Canada

Being a Parent

Chapter 1

Introduction

"THE CHILD IS FATHER OF THE MAN"[1] and the parents of the child have a great deal to do with this development.

The articles in this collection were all written for parents in an effort to help them with this difficult task. In them, Karl Bernhardt developed his philosophy about the nature of the child as a bundle of potentialities and about the important role that parents and other significant adults play in developing a healthy child. An important key to the interchange between parent and child is consistency of approach. Discipline must be logical with consequences following from the child's behaviour. The aim should be the development of an independently secure individual. All of these themes are introduced in the articles in this first chapter, and they will recur and be expanded throughout the book.

Tomorrow's citizens[2]

It is easy today to be pessimistic. World events and local happenings provide plenty of reasons for gloomy predictions. Suspicion, hate, discontent, crime, family breakdown, and many forms of maladjustment are not new but seem to be more apparent, although it may be that there is merely more concern about them and more publicity than previously.

There are, however, real reasons for hope and optimism, one of which is human flexibility. Man can learn to adjust to practically any situation. He is capable of solving his problems, even that most important problem of learning how to live at peace with himself and his neighbours. This flexibility is greatest during childhood. Although it is not inevitable or necessary, yet it is usual for flexibility to decrease as age increases.

Our hope, then, rests with tomorrow's citizens, today's children. It is trite but necessary to reiterate that what these citizens of tomorrow will be like depends on what happens to them today in our homes, schools, and communities.

It is difficult if not impossible to predict what the world will be like twenty years from now, but we can be sure of a few things. We can be sure, for instance, that there will be problems to solve, that there will be work to be done, that people will have to live together, and that their main goal will still be to find happiness in living. It is for these broad

1 W. Wordsworth, *My Heart Leaps Up When I Behold.*
2 K. S. Bernhardt, "Tomorrow's citizens," *Parent Educ. Bull.* 1947, no. 40, 2 – 5.

but important things that we seek to prepare our children. We can be sure that the world will continue to change and we can be fairly sure that the tempo of change will continue to increase. And so our children must be prepared for change and to be able to adjust to changes as they happen. This means that child training cannot be training in set and specific patterns but must be the development of an ability to deal adequately with varied and changing situations.

All of this is pretty general and speculative and you demand (as you should) more concrete and practical suggestions to help you to discharge your responsibilities as a parent, a teacher or a community leader. Might I, therefore, suggest some practical principles of child training?

EVERY CHILD HAS THE POTENTIALITIES FOR HAPPY, SUCCESSFUL LIVING

No child is ever doomed to a life of unhappiness or maladjustment because of his heredity. We should never use the excuse that the child was "born that way." It is true that there are limitations imposed by heredity in terms of academic ability, musical and artistic talent and the like. But it is not true that heredity is responsible for maladjustment, delinquency, or poor character. Those things are the products of learning and experience. No matter what equipment the child has by virtue of his heredity background, he is still capable of achieving a happy, useful, healthy life. This principle provides us with hope as well as challenge. No parent or teacher has the right to place the blame on biology. Every parent and teacher has the responsibility of providing every child with the kind of environment and experiences which will result in the achievement of happiness and efficiency in the business of living. For every child has to learn the essentials of the happy life.

CHILDREN NEED DIRECTION

No matter what kind of society the individual lives in, there will always be compulsions and restrictions. No one can live at peace with his neighbours without some curb on his freedom, for freedom in the sense of free expression of desires and individual wants is an impossibility. An important part of child training is the provision of the essential rules and regulations of civilized life. This does not mean that everything is decided for the child but it does mean that he is helped to accept external controls.

It is important that the child learn early that there are some things that are not done and others that must be done. The well-adjusted person is one who has learned to accept the necessary restrictions and compulsions of civilized living. There are a number of possible responses to frustration. Training and direction should be designed to help the child find the most desirable of these. For instance he can learn to escape by illness, day-dreaming, running away, neglect, or procrastination. He can use an emotional response, temper tantrums or tears. But if he is to be a useful citizen of tomorrow he must learn to accept the demands of his environment and live up to his responsibilities. The adult's job is to see that the child cannot escape without suffering the consequences of his failure.

IMPERSONAL CONTROLS ARE BETTER THAN PERSONAL DIRECTION

The usual and easier methods of directing the child are through personal appeals of various kinds – rewards, appeals to affection, disapproval, do this for me, mother will be angry or disappointed, to name a few. They are often successful in terms of immediate results, but they hinder the child from learning the meaning of necessary restrictions and compulsions. Part at least of the meaning of growing up is the acceptance of necessary patterns of civilized life not because someone wants us to behave that way but because it is the intelligent, sensible way to act.

Impersonal controls emphasize necessity, not how the parent or other adults feel about it. For instance, the child learns to go to bed at a certain time not merely because mother wants it that way but because he needs the sleep, or he learns to eat what is put before him not to please anyone but merely because it is meal time and this is the food provided. It is the parent's job to see that he accepts the necessary requirements of living or else suffers immediate and impersonal consequences.

EVERY EXPERIENCE CHANGES THE INDIVIDUAL

It is the everyday happenings that determine the individual's personality and character. This places a serious responsibility on parents, teachers, and others to provide the kind of environment which will be conducive to good personality development. Home, school, church, and community organizations can work together to build strong citizens of tomorrow.

The child needs a home in which he feels secure, in which he has a chance to work and play and satisfy his need for affection, advancement, and independence. He needs a school which takes into account his level of ability in a way that provides him with a feeling of achievement. He needs a community which is safe both physically and morally, and which provides him with opportunities for interesting activities. The child thus provided for does not have the time or the need to get into trouble.

THE HOME CLIMATE AFFECTS THE CHILD

Attitudes, moral standards, manners, ways of thinking, and patterns of behaviour are absorbed by the child from his social environment. Manners are caught not taught. Honesty is learned, if at all, in the everyday business of living rather than as a lesson. The intolerance we see in a child is a reflection of the same attitude in the adults with whom he lives.

What is usually called home influence is a complex of ways of living, thinking, and acting which the child accepts uncritically and weaves into the pattern of his personality. "Like father like son" is not so much an expression of heredity influence as an indication of the infectious nature of attitudes, standards, and patterns of behaviour.

There are apparent exceptions to this principle, for example the proverbial "bad" preacher's son. But sometimes the child fails to reflect the moral standards of the adult because there has been so much insistence on certain artificial standards that they have become distasteful to the child.

GROWING-UP TAKES A LONG TIME AND CANNOT BE HURRIED

In fact sometimes trying to push the child retards his development. It is often the ambitious parent who has the most trouble and disappointment. Hurrying the child or expecting him to act like an adult long before he is grown up is one sure way to produce difficulty.

Adjusting to our complex culture is a difficult and involved process. It takes years to learn. What we can and should look for is progress and improvement each year but certainly not perfection. Training in social adjustment, emotional expression, and independence should be progressive, extending over about twenty years. The best guarantee that the individual will be able to deal adequately with each new problem and situation is his proven ability in handling previous problems. We have learned that adjusting builds on previous experience and the success of any adjustment depends on what has gone before. That is why it is so important that the child be helped to manage the problems of his age.

Being a parent, teacher or any other adult who deals with young children brings great responsibility but it should also bring great joy. The parent who does not enjoy his role is probably not a good parent. Of course, there are worries and difficulties but watching the growth and development of a child and having a hand in shaping his or her personality and character should be one of the most satisfying of human experiences.

The "undone" things[3]

Being a good parent is an exacting, challenging occupation which requires study, planning, knowledge, understanding, and affection. Above all, it requires that we do not leave undone those things we ought to do. Perhaps this is where most of us fail most often.

One of the commonest of the undone things is a word of praise or commendation when a child has tried hard to do or learn something. By this we do not mean idle words of flattery but rather sincere expressions of praise that tell the child that we know he is making a real effort. It is often when a child has not quite succeeded that he needs words of encouragement which will keep him trying. This is the time when parents are apt to become impatient and to express criticism or disappointment; most of us have been guilty of this. But persistent effort is a requirement of learning, and nothing promotes persistence quite as much as a word of encouragement from someone for whom we have affection. The unsaid word of praise may say quite emphatically to a child that we do not care.

Some of us are afraid of spoiling our children, and because of this we often withhold words of affection or little treats that we might otherwise give. But children are not easily spoiled. Certainly they are not spoiled by knowing that their parents love them, or by the special treats which make some days remembered. However, they are spoiled when we do not see that they live up to necessary requirements or when we do things for them that they should do for themselves. So let us not

3 K. S. Bernhardt, "The 'undone' things," *Bull. Inst. Child Stud.*, 1958, 20 (3) , 1 - 2.

leave undone the little surprises and treats that gladden a child's heart, or leave unsaid those words of affection we want to say.

There is another kind of undone thing, the unfulfilled promise. It is easy to make promises but not always easy to keep them. We "forget," or circumstances change and make it difficult for us to do or provide what we have promised. A young child's trust in his parents is the foundation of his feelings and attitudes towards people in general. The stronger his trust in his parents the better is the foundation on which he builds his social attitudes. This is why parents should never leave undone those things which help to establish a child's sense of trust. If at all possible, promises must be kept. Perhaps we should be more careful about making them and only promise what we can be reasonably sure of providing.

Perhaps the most serious undone things are those involving our failure to provide an atmosphere that is conducive to healthy growth. I do not mean failure to provide physical comforts but rather failure to provide that feeling of acceptance and belonging that is as important as bread and milk. It is a combination of little things that say to a child, "We want you; we think you are important; we enjoy your presence; we are glad you are our child." But there is no formula or set of rules for conveying this message to children. It is a deep feeling of parenthood and humanity that is expressed through words, attitudes, and deeds in hundreds of ways.

The important things in bringing up children are often the little things – the words we use, the tone of our voice, the incidental events of the daily routine. It is always easier to neglect these little things than the more obvious and noticeable aspects of the job of parenthood, but it is the succession of these little things that make up the pattern of training and experience which is the material for personality building.

Building security in a changing world[4]

"We live in a changing world" is one of those familiar statements that we all accept without thinking very much about their meaning to us and to our children. Much the same can be said about "security." We

4 K. S. Bernhardt, "Building security in a changing world," *Bull. Inst. Child Stud.*, 1958, 20 (4) , 4 – 7.

talk about secure and insecure children, for instance, without exploring and questioning the meaning of the terms. This section proposes to examine the implications for parents and children of each of these concepts: "a changing world" and "security."

Change in our world is a fact with which we are all familiar. Some of us have lived longer and have seen a lot more change than others, but even our young people are aware of drastic changes in patterns and ways of living. Then, too, change is inevitable because we are the kind of people we are – learners, wanting to know and find out, and dissatisfied with our present knowledge.

Not all changes are necessarily good or desirable in terms of human welfare, mental health, or happiness. It is sometimes assumed that any technical advance is automatically good for people. We know, however, that the creation of a greater variety of "things," a so-called higher standard of living, does not necessarily mean greater human happiness or welfare. For example, when a housing development in Great Britain moved some hundreds of people from the worst possible dockyard slums into new homes in a new area, the physical surroundings were infinitely better, and yet there were symptoms of discontent. The happiness of these people depended on more than the physical conditions in their environment.

Each change in our world brings many other changes in its train. For example, the discovery of the wheel was a landmark in human progress; it started a whole series of changes that have gone on ever since. Thus the wheel has drastically changed our lives. This is the nature of any discovery, whether in the realm of technology or of human relations. Something is started that never stops. When we think of the series of changes brought about through the discovery of various forms of power and communication, we can even get a little frightened. We realize, sometimes, that we are living in the middle of rapid change and wonder if there is anything solid and permanent about us.

Now things seem to happen much more quickly in the field of technology than in the field of behaviour and human relationships. Although psychologists, sociologists, and anthropologists have been making a valiant effort to keep up or catch up, they still lag far behind. The reason for this is that the results of technological research are usable immediately: all we need is a machine and the knowledge of which knob to turn. But when discoveries about human nature and inter-personal relationships are made, we cannot merely build a box, complete with knobs and use this knowledge by turning a dial. We have to assimilate the knowledge and learn how to apply it to different individuals and situations. For this reason methods of child training are very slow to change. People must have time to test the effects of new approaches. In the meantime we hear, "Let's go back to the good old days when things weren't so difficult and we were surer of things," and "Back to the woodshed technique!" and "What's wrong with the use of fear? It gets better and quicker results than these new-fangled ideas." These statements are made, I think, because we feel more comfortable with the old and familiar.

What are some of the changes in family patterns and ways of living which we should understand? The emancipation of women was an important event. It has resulted in working mothers. It has changed ideas about family government and has led to confusion about democratic procedures in the family and about the meaning of "partnership" between husband and wife. Families have also become less permanent and more mobile. As a result of all these interconnected changes, families today do not provide the traditional solid base for emotional security.

Technological advances, too, have brought about great changes. Families do less of the necessary work within their own walls. Shorter working and longer playing hours affect family living patterns. Families are not the self-contained units that they once were; they lean more on the state and community for the care of their members, whether young, old, sick, disabled, or unhappy. One of the most unfortunate results of technological change on our way of living is the stress on "winning." Let us hope that at least for pre-school and young school children we may arrange experiences which leave out competition. Another undesirable result of these changes is the artificial stimulation of wants through advertising, which leads people today to emphasize values that are primarily materialistic.

What is the significance of all these changes? Family living and child care, being more complex, now require infinitely more thought, study, and effort. Forty years ago, Watson[5] talked of drilling into an individual, by repetition, a few basic patterns of thinking, feeling, and acting which would serve him for his lifetime. Now we try to help a child develop flexibility, understanding, an approach to problems, and a way of looking at meaning, purposes, values, and ideals.

These emphases in our training of children point directly to the core of our concept of security: that a secure individual, whether infant or

5 J. B. Watson, *Behaviorism*. Chicago: Univ. Chicago Press, 1924.

adult, is able to meet everyday situations with poise and equanimity. A secure person will adventure, launch forth into new experiences and tackle new problems. He does not need to be successful in all these ventures, but rather he accepts his failures along with his successes, in terms of his own efforts and in terms of the meaning of those failures in relation to those efforts. He moves on to each new problem with equanimity, meeting whatever comes, be it success or failure, with eagerness and confidence, and always accepting the results of his effort without distortion or regret. This, I think, is an individual who can live in any kind of world.

What is a suitable environment for this individual in the making? One requirement is a comfortable, stimulating, safe, and interesting setting for learning and living. This he needs particularly while he is young, as our knowledge of the relation between early experiences and later adjustment has shown us. While a child is young we establish for him a kind of bank account on which he can draw, and with which he can do all kinds of useful things, developing a trust in people. Such trust is greatly lacking today, whether between neighbours, between husbands and wives, or between parents and children. The adults who never let a child down, who are on his side, dependable and consistent, are paying into his bank account of trust towards other people. Nursery school teachers can contribute to this feeling of trust in the same way as parents, by believing in a child, by treating him always as an individual who can learn to do things for himself, who is going to be somebody. If adults really believe these things of a child, then he believes them too and develops the very necessary trust in himself and a feeling of confidence in his own worth.

Another aspect of security building is freedom from restraint, freedom to choose to do or not to do as he pleases, as a balance for the certain restraints necessary for the well-being of the child and of others. A child gains this sense of freedom through his creative efforts, through carrying out his own ideas in his own way. He gains a sense of freedom and a feeling of confidence in himself through his imaginative play; here he is free to pretend whatever he pleases, without being questioned as to its reality. When he says the chair is an automobile, then it is an automobile. We sometimes do not realize the important feeling of power a child gains from engaging in his own fantasy.

In addition to warm, accepting, dependable adults, and a certain freedom from restraint, a child needs stimulation in building skills. By this I mean not only physical skills, but also mental skills such as understanding, insight, and knowledge. To develop these skills a child needs to have plenty of problems with which he can struggle, and thus taste discovery and insight. As for imparting knowledge to a child, I wonder if we haven't been unnecessarily afraid lest a child's world of factual information be expanded with what we have said "belongs" to later years. Do we tell children of pre-school age enough facts? Our eyes and our ears will tell us what they are ready to "take"; if we give them the opening, they surely ask for knowledge. Security is thus strengthened by a solid foundation of facts which a child acquires not only through seeing, exploring, feeling, and doing, but also through listening to adults.

The picture would not be complete without reference to our well-known theory of consequences. The development of security is helped by the sure and steady acquisition of an understanding of the demands and restrictions of social living, of the satisfactions to be gained by fitting in with those demands, and of the disadvantages of trying to battle them.

The above points which I feel are essential for the building of security apply, of course, to both home and school. They may sound simple, but they are not easy to put into practice. There is always the temptation in home and in school to think of "how we look to others." It is nice to present a picture of smoothly running efficiency. However, we must always keep the child, rather than the picture, as the focus of our efforts. We may present an exterior which looks excellent, but fail to build security for each child in the school. A music group may seem charming, yet leave two or three children with the feeling of being pushed out and inadequate. A family can look wonderful yet fail to meet the needs of each member. We must always keep the individual child in mind and try to give him what he needs in order to grow secure.

What should we give them?[6]

Have you ever asked yourself: What's the best gift I can give my child – children? and wondered? Most parents have. And most parents have thought of the things that money will buy and have been

6   K. S. Bernhardt, "What should we give them?" *Bull. Inst. Child Stud.*, 1954, 16 (3), 1 – 4.

vaguely uneasy, as though there were something wrong, as though it wasn't good enough. And of course, it isn't, because the best gift for our children cannot be bought with money. Our best gift to them is love, understanding, and a pattern of living that they can accept.

There is abundant evidence that money and the things that money can buy are not enough and not particularly important. Let us take the case of the young man who had been given everything by his parents. They provided for him well – clothes, a generous allowance, a car to drive, travel, a University course – everything that money could buy. But his parents said he was not even grateful. Rather, he wasted his time – failed his University course and took no responsibility at home. His relations with his parents became uncomfortable for all and finally he left home. His father asked, "Where did we fail?" for he had that all too common parental feeling of failure and bewilderment. He felt that he had given his son everything. Actually he had given him everything except the things that mattered – affection, understanding, companionship and partnership in living.

Scientific studies have demonstrated what many people have known for years, namely that children need more than air to breathe, food, clothes, and shelter; they need a feeling of being wanted and accepted, understood and loved. And if they lack this feeling then they cannot grow and develop as they should, nor can they meet and learn to deal adequately with the problems of living. So when we ask ourselves what can we give our children, a part of the answer is clear. We can give them a feeling of being wanted and loved, accepted and understood.

Many parents are afraid of this doctrine. They are afraid because they do not want to be guilty of spoiling their children, of over-protecting them or smothering them in parental love. This is a legitimate fear. Most of us need to realize that it is possible to love our children without indulging, spoiling, or protecting them too much from those life situations in which they will learn to meet and deal with problems, to make decisions and face consequences. The concept of love does not mean that there should be no rules or requirements, no standards of behaviour or restrictions on their freedom. It does mean that we have to learn how to separate discipline and affection without letting one spoil the other. It means that the most effective discipline is impersonal – that the rules and regulations, requirements and restrictions grow out of situations and are dictated by those situations rather than by the whims of mother and father. The child, then, is required to do certain things and to refrain from doing other things, not because mother or father want it but because they are the sensible, reasonable, and necessary rules of the group and impersonal in the sense of being no one person's rules.

Parental love and acceptance do not depend on good behaviour; they are not rewards which the child is obliged to earn. The child needs this love and understanding most when his behaviour has not been good. But the love and understanding do not change either the rules or the consequences of not living up to the rules. This is what is meant by separating discipline and affection. Here is our adolescent, struggling with the problems of growing up, making mistakes, finding out that certain ways of behaving bring undesirable consequences. If ever loving and understanding parents are needed, it is at this time. But here his parents fail him; every mistake and every example of undesirable behaviour brings more parental disapproval. Finally, communication between parents and son is completely blocked, the son feeling that his parents neither love nor try to understand him, and the parents feeling that he is ungrateful, stubborn, and mean. And of course these feelings make it virtually impossible for the parents to help the son or the son to accept their help.

The other half of this best gift to children is a pattern of living. So much of what the child learns comes not from teaching but from example. Attitudes, standards of behaviour, ideals are largely absorbed by the child from those with whom he lives. He learns to be tolerant or intolerant, considerate or inconsiderate, courteous or discourteous, honest or dishonest from his family. This learning is not mechanical or automatic, but it is constant. The child accepts uncritically the patterns of behaviour of those for whom he has admiration and affection. Where admiration and affection are lacking, the child may actually reject the pattern of living, not because he does not like it but because he does not like his parents. It is a fortunate child who has parents who are mature, well-adjusted adults, for then he has a pattern of living which he can accept and from which he can benefit. This is a gift beyond price and more valuable than all the money in the world. How can we be sure that our children will receive this great gift? Here are some simple measures of maturity and some suggestions for improvement should we feel the need of it.

The mature adult lives in the present, lives easily, makes decisions promptly, accepts the consequences of his decisions and actions, meets and deals with his daily problems without rationalization or escape, has learned to manage and use his emotions, has a variety of interests and can entertain both himself and his friends, has goals, purposes, and ideals which lend meaning to his life, enjoys social contacts and has a number of friends and a sense of humour. All of these characteristics of the well-adjusted adult are products of learning, and all are subject to change and improvement. With practice anyone can improve in these aspects of behaviour. Let us examine some of them in more detail.

Living in the present seems so simple and sensible, and yet there are many people who have failed to learn to do so. A great teacher once said, "Take no thought for the morrow." What He was advising was the removal of those fears and tensions that arise from being concerned with the future. I am sure that the advice was not directed against planning for the future, but rather against being apprehensive of the future. The best preparation for any future event is to do the very best we can with the task in hand. Living in the past is just as crippling as living in the future. The past can teach us many lessons but the mature person does not waste time and effort in regretting the past nor does he live on his past achievements.

Living easily means minimizing the strains and stresses of everyday life. It is not advice against hard work, for "hard work never hurt anyone." But worry, strain, and emotional turmoil are certainly unhealthy. There are some things that are worth getting concerned about, but most of the things that irritate or annoy us, or produce worry and apprehension are trivial and unimportant. The healthy person does not let little things bother him. Living easily also means the ability to relax and to do so regularly. Perhaps for many parents the most important area for improvement is right here. So often parents become emotional about their contacts with their children – disturbed by things that are relatively unimportant – and need to learn to "take it easy."

Making decisions promptly and accepting the responsibility for such decisions is another important sign of maturity. Accepting the challenge of the everyday problems of living, dealing with them, and then abiding by the results without blaming other people form a mature and healthy pattern of living which children can learn to accept when it is apparent in their own home.

In this day of confused thinking and conflicting standards it is a fortunate child who has parents with standards and ideals to which they live up without fuss or display. Of course we do not want children to accept uncritically their parents' philosophy of life, but on the other hand children are much better off when they live with parents who do have such a philosophy and whose lives indicate an underlying meaning and purpose.

What should we give them? Certainly we owe them all the advantages that money can buy and that we can afford, but if we stop there we rob our children of some of the greatest assets for living. So in all our giving let's make sure we give them the essential gift – that of parents who love and try to understand them and who are evolving a pattern of living which the child will want to follow and which will stand him in good stead.

Chapter 2

The Home and the Family

ONE OF THE MOST IMPORTANT FACTORS in Karl Bernhardt's philosophy is the key role of the home in the development of the child. Throughout the articles in this section the pervasive tone is that of a democratic home in which each member of the family is accepted as an individual and in turn accepts his share of responsibility for the smooth running of the whole group.

Families are what we make them[1]

Nearly everyone belongs to two families – the one into which he was born and the one he helps to establish. What happens in the first determines to a large extent the success of the second. The experiences of the child in the family determine the attitudes of the child towards family life and to a considerable extent colour his thinking about the family that he will eventually help to build.

A good many people today are concerned about the future of the family. Some people talk about the possibility of almost complete family breakdown and disintegration. Such a pessimistic point of view is not, however, necessary, even though there have been rather far-reaching and in some ways serious changes in family structure. It is true that many things have happened to the family. It has decreased in size, has become more mobile, and is less permanent today because of the increase in separations and divorces. The individual depends on the community more than he did previously for such things as care of the sick and aged, for training and education of the child, and for recreation and entertainment. There is freer choice of marriage partners, less male dominance, and less economic dependence of woman. Inventions, gadgets, and many details of housekeeping have increased the complexity of the picture. These and a variety of other circumstances have brought about important changes in the general structure of the family.

It is difficult to evaluate what has happened and is happening in the family and what might be done to strengthen and preserve it as an institution. We hear and read many suggestions. There is the return to the "good old days" – the reinstating of customs and attitudes of a previous age. Of course this is usually not possible; too much has happened

1 K. S. Bernhardt, "Families are what we make them," *Bull. Inst. Child Stud.*, 1949, no. 45, 6–10.

in the meantime, and the old customs no longer fit the new family and the new family environment. A second suggestion is to remove the cause of our present problems. If for instance the automobile is the contributing factor in some of our difficulties, then remove the automobile. But the solution is never as simple as that. It isn't removal of the cause but readjustment of the total picture that is required. A third suggestion takes the form of simple rules and formulae – for example, the husband should bring his wife candies and flowers on special occasions. The papers and magazines stress this approach. But rules and formulae rarely get close to the basic attitudes involved. A fourth possibility is education for family life, i.e. the adequate preparation of the boy or girl for the responsibilities of family life. This includes the building up of attitudes, ideas, and skills that will enable them to do an effective job as husbands and wives and parents when it is their turn to establish new families. Related to this is a fifth suggestion which includes the formulation of values, objectives, and a philosophy of life to fit the changing society in which we live, for example the determination of what the family can provide in the way of emotional satisfaction and security. This might be called the affectional function of the family – the provision of companionship, affection, intimacies, solid human relationships that are dependable. This is possible even when the members of the family have many interests outside the home, but it is made easier and more meaningful when there is sharing of experiences of work and play, planning, worries, and problems.

The modern family, the family of the present and the future, could be called the companionship family in which there is a close, warm relationship between members. The family has become even more important than formerly as a setting for emotional expression – a place where formal requirements are not so prominent and where the individual may be accepted "as is" without being on display. It should also be a place where he can express and hear indications of affection and understanding, where there can be sympathetic responsiveness. It should be a centre of mutual helpfulness where common experiences and the practice of democratic living are shared. This implies a change of emphasis from the externals to the important features of human relationships within the family. It seems to be true that people demand more from the family today than in the past and for this reason there is more disappointment and frustration when the family fails to provide what is expected.

The intimate relationships involved in marriage and family life seem to involve at least three possibilities, with perhaps many variations and degrees: (1) a dominance-submission relationship, (2) an equality relationship, and (3) a condition in which there is no real interaction but merely separate individuals living in the same place. We may be able to gain some insight into the factors which make for an effective family life if we look in turn at these three possibilities.

In the dominance-submission relationship one individual is dominant and the other or others submissive. This is the traditional dictatorship family. It has enjoyed many years of acceptance as a well-established social norm and is slow to change. There are many vestiges of this idea left in the modern family but they are not always recognized for what they are. If the wife accepts the position of inferiority and the dominance of the husband, there is rarely any open conflict. But resentment and smoldering rebellion which, of course, may break out into open conflict, can and often do result. This conflict can only be resolved in two ways – a change from male dominance to some other relation or a reacceptance of the submissive role by the wife. This type of relationship can work in the opposite direction as well, with the wife dominant and the husband submissive, but this reversal of roles has not the sanction of convention and is usually the target of ridicule with resulting loss of respect by the submissive husband.

The second possibility – the equality relationship – is really one of alternate dominance and submission. It is much more difficult to manage, but when made to work is much more rewarding. The main technique here is compromise – a mutual giving up for a common goal, a goal accepted by both. This requires a good deal of discussion and threshing out of difficulties and differences of opinion, and this in turn requires the kind of maturity and objectivity that is regrettably rare. There is more chance of conflict because agreement is required, whereas the dominance relationship merely requires submission with or without agreement.

At the present time we seem to be in the process of transition from the traditionally male-dominated to the equality relation family. Like most transitions it has its difficulties. We sometimes see a mixture, an attempt at equality but a reversion to the dominance-submission picture in certain areas such as finance. Here the husband makes the decisions, manages the money of the family, and doles out a certain amount to the wife. Or we see a kind of division of responsibility rather than a sharing, which is sometimes expressed as "I don't interfere in your work, you shouldn't interfere in mine."

The equality relation requires an acceptance of the idea of equality. This is, however, never completely attained, so it usually results in shifting roles, and division of responsibility and of labour and areas. The more areas there are in the family situation for joint responsibility, planning, and agreement, the more effective the marriage relationship seems to be. The idea of co-operation and joint planning and agreement through discussion is not by any means new, but the actual carrying out of the idea requires more training and practice than most of us have had. It is the basic idea of democratic living which we have generally accepted intellectually even though we have difficulty in putting it into practice.

The third possibility – individuals living together without the development of any pattern – does occur, but it is an ineffective marriage relationship. Equality is assumed without either the technique of compromise or the acceptance of common purposes. Such a marriage is full of conflict possibilities but provides no basis for a solution.

In considering family life and relationships within the family we should not overlook the children. The family should fulfil two purposes: (1) provide emotional satisfactions and fulfilment for husband and wife and (2) a training ground for the children. We are sure that the equality relationship on the democratic pattern provides the best atmosphere for the training of the child, and look forward to a more effective practice of this democratic philosophy in the future. This will only happen when more and more children have a chance to learn how to live in a democratic way. The family can provide the setting.

The democratic family has a number of characteristics. First, there is respect for individual personality: the person is more important than anything else – family reputation, money, or good housekeeping. Then there is the importance of individual choice and decision. The individual must have plenty of opportunities to learn to choose and to experience the results of such choices. Still another aspect is the technique of discussion and compromise. We still have a lot to learn about this technique, but one essential is the removal of emotional appeals and adherence to set ideas. It only works when the persons concerned are able to look at the ideas and point of view of others as something to consider and evaluate rather than merely something to refute.

Many families today are trying a device that can be called the family council. This is a democratic assembly within the family in which the various points of view of its members including even those of the young children are expressed and listened to. It is a family forum in which decisions are made which affect the behaviour of the members of the group. Almost anything related to family living can be and should be a subject of discussion. Matters of money, leisure time activities, hours, use of family possessions are only a few of the things that can be thrashed out by the family in session. At first the young child is mainly a spectator, but gradually he becomes a participating member of the council. His presence should be salutary, for some parents would hesitate to be emotional and unreasonable in their approach to problems if they realized that the child is acquiring his patterns of behaviour from what he sees and hears. Gradually the child is helped to express his point of view as well as to listen to that of the other members of the family. One of the real difficulties is the child's lack of knowledge and experience, but when we understand that he can only acquire that knowledge and experience by practice we see how important it is for him to have a chance to participate. It is hoped that the child will gradually see that there are considerations beyond his own personal feelings and satisfactions. In other words he will learn to think in terms of the good of the group rather than in purely selfish terms. He will learn also that social living always means rules and regulations, or at least that some rules and regulations are essential to happy peaceful living with other people. We assume that the child will become a more truly social being by seeing something of the process by means of which the rules are made, rather than by merely learning to accept blindly what he is told to do.

The family is so valuable and fulfils so much that is basic in human life that it is sure to persist – changed in some of its surface characteristics but fundamentally the same in the sense that it satisfies the basic needs of the individual and provides an emotional anchor in a changing world. The changes that have taken place and continue to take place in the family bring us nearer to the equality relationship, the democratic pattern, and the companionship family.

The companionship family puts more emphasis on the problem of human relations and less on externals. Clinicians, social workers, and others working with people in family situations have been emphasizing the importance of feelings of belonging, acceptance, and security in social relations. This emphasis has led to a more careful scrutiny of this factor of human relations in the family. We are beginning to realize that the family has a large and important part to play in the emotional development of its members; it can provide freedom for personality development. But where there is more freedom and more intimacy there is also the need for more skill in using that freedom and in managing the intimacies. The family can and should be a place where individuals learn the meaning of mutual helpfulness and sharing, and where they can learn to practice and feel comfortable with the techniques of democratic living.

What a good home is like[2]

Here we present a list of some of the things which make the kind of home that is a good place to grow up in.

1   The parents are genuinely interested in their children and show it by their enjoyment in working and playing with them. They listen when their children try to tell them about what happened during the day. The supper table is a place for all members of the family to enjoy each other and to talk about the things in which they are interested.

2   The children feel that they belong and are secure. They know that their parents will try to understand them and treat them as persons who matter. They know that their time and interests are respected and accepted. They think of the home as theirs, not just as their parents'.

3   The children like to bring their friends home because they are welcomed and have a good time. The child selects his own friends and the parents don't criticize the friends after they are gone.

4   The parents realize that no two children are alike. They see their own children as individuals, each with his own strengths and weaknesses.

5   When parents lose their tempers, as they sometimes do, they snap out of it quickly. They let bygones be bygones and don't hold the child's sins over his head. The parents are not over-anxious or surprised when their children display faults or make mistakes. They are fair and reasonable, willing to listen to the child's side of the story.

6   The parents can say "You must" or "You may not" when the situation calls for it but they are very careful that it isn't an expression of authority only but a necessary and reasonable "must" or "must not." At the same time they are quick to see when a child has good enough judgment to be his own boss and to give him as much responsibility as he is ready to carry.

2   K. S. Bernhardt, "What a good home is like," *Parent Educ. Bull.*, 1940, no. 9.

7 The parents have a set of values which sets the tone of the whole home. They have the courage to stick to their values and to practice them. They believe in the intrinsic worth of every human being, which means that they are sympathetic and considerate of all the people with whom they come in contact.

Reducing family tensions[3]

There are many reasons why the family should function without tension and conflict. Not the least of these reasons is the healthy growth and development of the children. No child can develop in a healthy way in an emotional climate characterized by strain and tension.

Of course there will be many differences of opinion and clashes of judgment and standards in the normal family, but these need not develop into areas of strain and tension. For the effective functioning of the family these differences must be resolved in a way that is satisfactory to all concerned. Hard feelings, resentments, irritations, and misunderstandings must be dealt with in such a way that they are removed before they become smoldering areas of family tension.

There is one simple principle which helps greatly in this matter. It is the principle of prompt and adequate treatment of difficulties before they have a chance to become serious. Often family tensions develop merely because things that are trivial in themselves are allowed to cumulate until they become major areas of misunderstanding and conflict. In fact, most serious family difficulties are of this nature. Sometimes the large and important issues are dealt with as they arise but the little annoying differences are allowed to pile up until they have become serious sources of tension. The home, to be effective, must be an essentially happy place for all its members. When nagging little irritations are allowed to persist this happiness is destroyed.

Some common areas of conflict in the family might be mentioned, but it should be kept in mind that each family situation is unique and what causes trouble in one may not be a difficulty in another at all.

Many family tensions arise from inconsistent application of discipline. When the child cannot be sure what is demanded of him, or when the

3 K. S. Bernhardt, "Reducing family tensions," mimeo., 1950.

demands differ from day to day, almost every small issue becomes a major battle ground. There are some things that can be settled once for a period of time and need not be a daily cause of argument. Such things are the regular requirements of everyday activities, such as bedtime, time and place for homework, music lessons and practice, home chores, and the care of possessions. The regulation of the child does not need to be, indeed should not be, a series of daily battles over the same issues. The school-age child can be helped to accept the necessary, reasonable, and sensible requirements of daily activities, but he can only accept these willingly and cheerfully when the requirements are consistent, reasonable, and minimal.

Another related factor is the quality of the control used. When this control is highly personal, that is, depends on the whims of the adult, it can easily become an emotional matter of coaxing, arguing, and resentment. And when emotion creeps into the picture, tensions multiply. Tears, temper tantrums, hurt feelings are the products of a personal method of control.

The balance between the two major functions of parenthood – discipline and companionship – should be mentioned also. When the main or only contacts between the parent and the child are for the purpose of control and discipline, it is easy for the relationship to degenerate into a constant battle. But when the parent and the child enjoy the times when they have a chance to share each other's company, the strains and tensions are not so frequent or so serious.

Many difficulties arise in the family because the two parents fail to agree on the things that are required of the child, the techniques to be used, or the kind of treatment to be given to the child. It is one of the happy features of parenthood that there are usually two parents to share the experience with each other. When the responsibilities and pleasures of the job are actually shared and when the partners – mother and father – can agree on the major issues, it can be a happy, satisfying experience. When, however, mother and father are not in essential agreement, it can be disturbing to both the parents and the children. A difficult situation can arise when the child learns to play one parent against the other, to gain permission from one and not from the other for some activity, but this can be avoided by sufficient discussion and agreement on essentials.

The use of family possessions, television for example, frequently leads to difficulty. This usually calls for family discussion and agreement about times and programmes so that inconvenience to individual members of the family can be avoided. Family discussion is one of the best techniques of avoiding problems and of settling them when they arise if the family can learn to participate without too much emotion. Family discussion, however, is itself a technique which requires considerable skill and training. It can easily become a battle in which individual members of the family try to convince other members of the family that they are right and the others wrong. It depends on a spirit of mutual trust, confidence, and respect which frequently must be cultivated carefully because it does not happen automatically.

Every society needs rules and regulations, but such rules and regulations work best when they are derived by co-operative means and are enforced with mutual trust and responsibility. Rules that are handed down in an autocratic way by the parent are themselves causes of tension and difficulty, but rules that are agreed on after sufficient discussion as necessary and sensible are more easily accepted and observed. So we see that rules can be a kind of lubrication that keeps the wheels of the family machinery turning smoothly, or they can be sources of strain and family tension. It all depends on the general spirit of the home, the way in which the rules are derived, and how they are enforced.

Family tensions can arise from differing standards of behaviour. The standards of performance often required by parents in such things as cleanliness, tidiness, noise, and other related aspects of family life often tend to be too strict. Many children fail to see the importance of so much emphasis on these features. There is often need for the parents to revise their expectations in the light of the age of the child and his present way of looking at things. Many battles could be prevented if parents could learn to accept lower standards of performance in some activities.

Again, many tensions could be avoided if parents be more realistic in their ambitions for their children. Many parents expect the impossible in terms of school work and other related activities. Many a family tension has arisen from the almost insatiable ambition of the parent. What some parents need to realize is that it is not possible for their children to stand first in their classes or beat the neighbours' children.

Time is often a source of dissension in the family. When members of the family are late for meals or fail to arrive home when they should, scolding, emotional scenes, and battles may result. It is important that the child learn to consider other people in his daily activities, and important that he learn to manage time well enough that he does not disrupt the group. The child can be helped in this learning if there is a basic regularity about the affairs of the household – meals on time, etc. He can be helped also to know exactly what is required of him in this regard, and what to expect if he fails to live up to such necessary family rules.

Some family tensions arise from failure on the part of the parents to allow the child sufficient privacy, by their persistence in prying into every minute of his day. The growing child needs to have some time to himself, time that he does not have to account for in detail. He also needs some privacy in possessions, things he can call his own and which are safe from interference by the rest of the family.

The child who has a family in which he feels he belongs, in which he is accepted and at home, is fortunate because his emotional climate is one in which healthy growth and development are possible. Tensions, battles, and misunderstanding do not provide the child with the kind of environment in which he can learn how to live. Family life does not need to be a series of battles and difficulties. It can run smoothly if parents will take the time to plan a reasonable routine and a set of requirements that the child can accept and live up to without too much difficulty.

The family at work and play[4]

In every family there is a certain amount of work which must be done in order to provide a happy, smooth-running living situation. There are two ways of looking at this work – first, how to get it done and, secondly, how to use the situation as a training ground for the children in the family. If we as parents think only of getting the work done, then probably the easiest solution would be to do it ourselves and not bother the children. But, if we think of the importance to the child of learning to accept responsibility and fulfil it, then we must consider the second view.

When thinking of the work of the family and the child's place in the picture there are a number of important objectives that should be kept in mind:

1 The child should feel that he belongs in the family – that he is a member of the family and as such has a part to play in the necessary work of the household.

4 K. S. Bernhardt, "The family at work and play," mimeo., 1950.

2   The child should learn to think of the work he does not as mother's work or father's work but *his* work.

3   The child should get an early start in healthy work habits and work attitudes.

4   The child should avoid the attitude of work snobbery and learn to think of no work as beneath his dignity or that some work is necessarily woman's work.

5   The child should learn not just to do work, but to accept the idea that it is his work – his own responsibility. It is not necessary that he learn to enjoy all work but it is important that he learn to accept the work as necessary and also that he learn to do the work adequately.

DESIRABLE ATTITUDES TOWARDS WORK

1   A willing and cheerful acceptance of responsibility for doing work that must be done.

2   An attitude of co-operation in working agreeably with others.

3   An attitude of interest either in the purpose of the work or in the work activity itself.

4   A willingness to evaluate fairly one's own accomplishments and to welcome constructive criticism from others.

5   An acceptance of all kinds of work and no "work snobbery."

WHAT ARE GOOD HABITS?

1   Working while you work – separating work and play – concentrating on the task at hand.

2   Intelligent persistence – effort sustained long enough to make progress.

3   Doing work well – attaining a sufficient level of proficiency.

4   Dependability – self-directed activity without the need for constant check-up.

REGULATING WORK CONDITIONS:
THE PARENTS' RESPONSIBILITY

1   Some general considerations: the tasks should be related to the child's present ability. Tasks that are too difficult lead to dawdling and other problems. The child should be helped to understand what is required and also the meaning and importance of the work itself. He needs some training and guidance in how to go about the tasks, but at the same time he should have considerable freedom in working out the details for himself.

2   Organizing a work routine: the planning of the work of the home is best done as a co-operative activity with all members participating. When the child has some part in the division of work and some voice in his own share of it he accepts the responsibility more readily and seriously. This planning should be done at intervals of about a week with considerable variety introduced into the child's share. A family notice board can be employed as an impersonal reminder of each member's current work. Planning the use of time is an important phase of the training of the child in good work habits. Such planning includes blocks of time for both work and play.

3   Conditions favourable for efficient work: the provision of a place for the child to do such tasks as his school work is desirable. This place should ensure a minimum of distractions, and interruptions and the fear of interruptions should be controlled.

4   Parental example and attitudes: perhaps the condition that exerts the most influence on the child's learning is the example he sees in his parents. He learns cheerful acceptance of responsibility, prompt and efficient performance of tasks, and an attitude of co-operation if this is the kind of pattern that is set by his parents.

THE FAMILY AT PLAY

One of the greatest influences on the mental hygiene of the family is the feeling of companionship and understanding which comes from play together. Because so many of the parental contacts with the children are of necessity for routine and regulation, it is important from the child's point of view that some contacts with the parents be less serious and aimed at mutual enjoyment. Many children who have splendid persons for parents have never discovered it because the only time they see their parents is when they are being corrected, criticized, and told to do or not to do something. There is great value in the sharing of enjoyable experiences. Of course it should be recognized that the child should have interests outside the home and that he should not be expected to spend all his leisure time with the family, or become too dependent on the family for all his leisure time activities. It should also be recognized that forced participation may result in a lack of spontaneity and enjoyment.

When one looks back on his early family life and seeks for those moments of enjoyment and the features of that life which made it so pleasant and valuable, one thinks immediately of the times when the family was in a festival mood – when all members of the family played together in a spirit of equality and comradeship. Such times cannot occur every day, but they can be more frequent than is the case in most families today.

There are many kinds of family play. The examples given here are only suggestions: outings, excursions, picnics, theatre, games, reading aloud, crafts, hospitality. There are many more and the effective family employs a variety of enjoyable group activities.

The family is the training ground for living. The habits, attitudes, and skills acquired in the family form the foundation of the individual's adjustment to life. What the boy or girl learns or fails to learn in the family influences how he will adjust to the complex business of living in a very complex world.

The mental health of the individual, his happiness and efficiency in the business of living, depends to a great extent on the kind of experiences he has in his family. Many of the emotional immaturities and maladjustments of adult life can be traced to these experiences.

Practically all parents want to provide for their children the kind of training which will make them capable of living a happy, full life. It is not easy to set up a family which functions smoothly and many parents fail, not for want of trying but rather for want of knowledge and thought.

Chapter 3

The Parents

THE KEY TO ANY SUCCESSFUL SCHEME of discipline for the child is the role of the parents. In this chapter Karl Bernhardt emphasizes the importance of both mother and father in the family situation. He also outlines the values of a democratic atmosphere in the home. Parental responsibilities are not easy and the parent should not be discouraged by the many setbacks.

What it means to be a good parent[1]

Being a good parent is a real challenge for it is something that does not just happen. It requires effort, study, and a number of attitudes and personality traits which can be cultivated. It takes love, patience, clear objectives, intelligence, skill, and knowledge.

PARENTS SHOULD LOVE THEIR CHILDREN

Although it is taken for granted by most parents that they should love their children, there are some aspects of parental love which need to be discussed. One of the most important features of child training is the provision of a basis for the feeling of belonging, of being wanted, accepted, and loved. The child who does not feel wanted and loved is the child who is likely to develop emotional quirks and present behaviour problems that may be difficult to deal with. But loving one's children does not mean either indulgence and spoiling or using affection as a method of control. The two main functions of parenthood, affection and discipline, should be kept separate and distinct. This is not easy. It is all too simple to use affection as a tool of control, to make affection appear as a reward for good behaviour. This can both cheapen affection and make discipline less adequate than it might be. Parents should love their children – by all means! But that love should not depend on good behaviour; it should stand as a solid unchanging background of parent-child relations. Happy is the child who feels that he is wanted and loved – happy because he is living in an atmosphere conducive to healthy learning and development.

THE CHILD NEEDS TWO PARENTS

Many a father has the idea that there is little place for him in the early years of the child's development. This idea not only robs them of much

1 K. S. Bernhardt, "What it means to be a good parent," *Bull. Inst. Child Stud.*, 1950, no. 47, 6 – 9.

pleasure but it also robs the young child of a contact which he needs. Mother, of course, has a central place in the development of the young child. She is entrusted with most of the care and develops a more intimate relationship with the child. But father has a place too, and the child's life is not complete without his companionship. Mother and father are partners and can help each other by taking time to discuss their hopes and fears, their plans and techniques, and to find through such discussions clearer ideas, a more objective attitude, and a better plan for dealing with the everyday problems of parenthood.

BEING A GOOD PARENT REQUIRES PATIENCE

It takes time for the child to learn. A large part of the parents' job is to arrange opportunities for learning, and then allow the child to use these opportunities. The rhythm of a child's activity is not as rapid as that of an adult, nor is his muscular co-ordination as well developed. One can frequently observe the impatience of adults with young children and their consequent attempts to hurry them. This is true in many such situations as dressing, washing, and eating, and often gives rise to that unfortunate but common habit of nagging. All that is needed here is a realization that the child is naturally slow and awkward in his movements, that he is learning, and that he cannot be expected to handle these activities as efficiently as he will later. One must be willing to wait.

It takes a long time to produce a mature adult. A very common parental mistake is that of expecting too much from the child too soon. The five-year-old should not be expected to act like an adult. Frequently parents are heard to say to their children, "Don't be childish." But, why shouldn't a child act like a child? It takes a lot of parental patience to guide the fumbling, awkward behaviour of the child without pushing or hurrying him.

Another place where parental patience is needed is in the inevitable comparisons of one's own child with others. Family pride is involved, for when a parent hears that the neighbour's child is developing faster than his own he is tempted to blame his child or try to hurry him. We all need to be reminded frequently that children differ greatly in their tempo of learning and development. Comparisons are dangerous and family pride can be an enemy of effective child training.

KNOW YOUR GOALS

Know what you want the child to learn and why. Half the battle of effective guidance is won by knowing what is desirable. The simplest and soundest method of deciding on the best course to follow with children is to decide first what the end result is to be, what kind of person we are trying to produce. What do we want? Is it a child who always does as he is told? A child who is well behaved? Or are we interested in goals that go beyond the present and into the future? Of course every parent has to decide these things for himself, but I would suggest that it is necessary to consider a long-range goal such as the production of a well-adjusted adult, for when we think in terms of the future of the child we use different techniques and emphasize different things. When we think in terms of the present only, we tend to use methods which get immediate results, but when we take the long-range view we tend to select methods which aid the learning and development of the child.

Most people would agree that the best goal for parents to keep in mind is the kind of individual the child is to be – an individual who is self-disciplined, capable of running his own life satisfactorily, capable of adjusting to the ever-changing world in which he will live. If such a goal is accepted, it means that we take pains to arrange opportunities for the child to learn how to decide things for himself, that we help him to take more and more responsibility for himself, that we help him to manage a gradually increasing freedom.

Being thoroughly aware of our goals, we plan a programme of child training which helps and does not hinder the child in his progress towards maturity. We have a progressive attitude, aware that the child does not stand still but is always learning, growing, and developing, and we shape our techniques to this changing picture. What the child learns and how he learns rather than mere obedience or good behaviour, become central.

KNOW HOW CHILDREN LEARN

In order to direct learning it is necessary to know how learning takes place. Some simple aspects of the process can be mentioned here. Learning requires motivation. There has to be a reason, and the most dependable motives are the child's own needs and wants. To learn the child must put forth effort, try out various things, taste the feelings of success and failure, and discover what works and what does not work. Mistakes are an inevitable and necessary part of learning, and learning is often slow and gradual with many set-backs and periods without progress. Learning is most efficient when the results of the child's efforts are immediate and consistent. Thus, perhaps the most important principle for the parent to keep in mind is consistency – always the same result following the same kind of behaviour.

KNOW WHAT YOU CAN EXPECT
FROM THE CHILD

This requires careful and frequent observation. It seems strange to tell parents that they need to know their child better, but it is advice which is frequently needed. Parents tend to make one or other of the following mistakes: either they do not expect enough of the child, or they expect too much. Perhaps the first is more frequent, i.e. not realizing that the child is ready for wider freedom and more responsibility and thus treating a four-year-old like a two-year-old. The parents have failed to keep up with the child's development. The opposite side of the picture is the parent who is ambitious for his child and tries to push him beyond his years and his present capacities. The six-year-old child is expected to behave like a twelve-year-old. The important thing is to study the child as objectively as possible to learn what he is capable of and when he is ready for new experiences and new learning.

PARENTS NEED TO PLAN

Planning is based on objectives and knowledge of what and how the child learns. It is essential to provide the opportunities for learning when the child is ready. Teaching and guidance of the child mean arranging learning opportunities. A child can acquire good eating habits, for instance, when the eating situation is planned with suitable furniture, utensils, and a consistent, regular routine. Early in his development, and the earlier the better, the child should learn that living makes demands on him, that there are requirements which must be met. These requirements should be planned by the parents with sufficient care to ensure that they are reasonable and suited to the child's stage of development and thus within his capacity to perform. These requirements should be understood by the child and be seen as necessary parts of the day's activities rather than as whims of parents. The child learns to accept these requirements when they are planned to be regular, consistent, reasonable, and just.

Planning includes arranging both routine requirements and free play situations. Play is an essential part of the child's activity. It provides relief from the required routine activities and is essentially a free activity with no compulsions and little outside regulation. Planning for it includes providing place, time, materials, ideas, and occasional companions. The busy child is usually the happy child and the learning child.

PROVIDE WHOLESOME PATTERNS FOR IMITATION

Young children imitate what they see and absorb what they hear. The attitudes, ideas, opinions, prejudices, and behaviour of parents are picked up by their children. Likes and dislikes, interests, manners and morals are learned mainly by this process of imitation and absorption. The unwitting influences of parents are often more important than the intentional techniques. A parent should be a healthy well-adjusted person who lives the kind of life he is trying to produce in the child.

PARENTHOOD REQUIRES STUDY AND KNOWLEDGE

Being a good parent requires constant study and learning. Good parents realize that knowledge has advanced in the field of child training as in other fields and that new and better methods of guiding children have been developed. The good parent is a learner. He is open-minded and critical. He is willing to be experimental in his attitude and approach to his problems as a parent. He takes advantage of the accumulating knowledge of child development and discusses the methods and techniques of training with others. He is observant, thoughtful, and flexible. Above all he wants his children to grow up, to advance towards the goal of maturity. Being a good parent requires study, knowledge, and patience; it is never boring. Nothing can be more exciting and satisfying than to watch and guide the development of a child. To see the child becoming a happy, well-adjusted adult, taking his place in the world and meeting his problems with courage and intelligence is the only reward the parent requires.

The father in the family[2]

When father loses his position in the family as head of the household he seems to become a kind of fifth wheel. He is, of course, still important as a wage earner and as a court of final appeal in matters of discipline, but in the intimate details of family life he is often a bystander. This is,

2 K. S. Bernhardt, "The father in the family," *Bull. Inst. Child Stud.*, 1957, 19 (2) , 2 – 4.

however, not true of all fathers; many have become more intimately involved in family activities. Some are entertaining story-tellers for toddlers, others are sources of information for eager school-age researchers, and many are good baby-sitters, adept at changing diapers and preparing formulas. Fathers are certainly not left out of the picture in all families, but their role needs to be more clearly defined and understood.

To understand father's place in the family requires some discussion of family organization and especially of the changes that have been taking place in the management of the home. For some time now we have been in the midst of a transition from an authoritarian to a democratic form of family. In this change father has discovered that he is not alone on his throne. When the promise to obey dropped out of some marriage ceremonies we indicated that we were trying to think of marriage as a partnership of equals. Such changes in attitude and approach to an institution as complex as marriage take time; the traditions of centuries do not disappear overnight. An equality relationship requires techniques to resolve differences in opinion and methods. One such technique is discussion culminating in agreement which is usually a compromise. Most of us find that discussion often deteriorates into argument. Many of the traditional patterns of the authoritarian family persist and confuse the picture of a family based on a husband-wife equality partnership. For instance, in many families father is still the sole authority on the management of the family income and doles out a fixed amount for the other partner to manage.

Social change and transitions from one pattern of living to another are often confusing and disruptive. This seems to be true of the rapid changes that are taking place in family life. Such changes may run contrary to the deeply ingrained habits of thinking and feeling that colour and help to determine the way we behave. When we take the time to examine and evaluate the goals and principles that guide our behaviour some of this confusion disappears.

One of the comforting aspects of a husband-wife "partnership" is the mutual help and support possible to each partner. For example, mother and father can help each other greatly by discussing the children's development and the methods used in their training. It is extremely important that the requirements enforced in the family be consistent. Father and mother should make the same demands of the children, and this can only follow considerable discussion and agreement between the parents as to what is reasonable and what can be ignored. It often happens that father tends to be either more demanding or more lenient than mother. This difference in treatment can not only confuse the child but destroy effective training.

Mother and father can also help each other to attain a more objective view of the children's development. Mother deals every day with the intimate details of the children's behaviour and it is sometimes difficult for her to maintain the necessary perspective. Small difficulties may loom large and obscure more important issues. Through discussion some of these daily annoyances slip into their rightful place and cease to be so important or irritating. Father usually has the advantage of being less emotionally involved in the daily happenings and may thus be able to bring a different point of view to the discussion. Of course, he helps by being sympathetic and supportive, but he can also provide greater objectivity and a long-range perspective.

Fathers have a greater chance today to participate in the intimate life of the family because they have more leisure time than formerly. The five-day work week means that most fathers have two days at home and can be available some of the time to relieve mother of the supervision of the children. If father accepts this opportunity it can pay big dividends. He can get to know his children better, and they can get to know their father. He can be more intelligent in discussions about the children and can become more understanding of the daily problems and difficulties that beset the mother. The relief offered to mother is by no means the smallest dividend. She really can do a much better job of supervising her children if she has some time free of the responsibility. Some families have discovered how valuable it can be to all concerned to plan a regular time each week when father takes charge of the children and mother can do whatever she likes.

Children learn the meaning of marriage and family life chiefly through observing their own parents. It is a fortunate child that gathers his knowledge of the meanings of marriage and family life from parents who enjoy each other and illustrate a happy and effective partnership. Boys and girls develop their ideas of the roles of men and women in our society from seeing how their own parents behave. Not the least, then, of father's responsibilities is to provide his children with a picture of mature, adult behaviour. In some families, as the children get older, father takes more responsibility for the boys and mother for the girls. It is doubtful whether this is desirable. Boys need companionship with both parents; girls can profit from contact with father as well as with mother.

Father has an important place in the family. True, his role is no longer that of a dictator, benevolent or otherwise, but it can be far more important: that of a participating member of a partnership, an understanding friend and guide of his children, an interesting, entertaining member of a group, and an example of adult adjustment. It is very easy for father to be left out of important family happenings, especially when the children are young or if he lets himself become merely the family banker and judge. To be a functioning father requires planning, thought, and effort, but the rewards are great. The day is fast disappearing when fathers are cast in the role of Santa Claus or bogey man. They are either relegated to the background or they take an active contributing place in family life. Today's families still need fathers, and fathers are finding deep satisfaction in their role.

Parent-child relationships[3]

Nearly every parent loves his children, but in many cases misunderstandings, hard feelings, and open conflict occur between parent and child. It would seem that love is not sufficient to produce a happy parent-child relationship. What else is needed? Among other things we would say that common sense, knowledge of what can be expected of the child, reasonableness, patience, and intelligence are necessary.

Very often good parent-child relationships are hindered by the use of affection as a method of control. Mother and/or father should not try to get the child to do something by indicating that they will love him more if he does, since affection dependent on good behaviour is always a mistake. It may be that the child will be good in order to be loved but his idea of the meaning of love is distorted as a result. It is very important that the child feel secure in the affections of his parents; any insecurity in this area may have serious results. Affections, then, should never be used as a lever to move the child; he needs to feel that no matter what happens there is a solid emotional anchor, that his mother and father will love him always.

The most important single factor in the development of children is a good relationship with their parents. The child needs to feel that there is at least one solid dependable fact in the changing confusion of his

3   K. S. Bernhardt, "Parent-child relationships," *Parent Educ. Bull.*, 1946, no. 38, 1–3.

social relationships, that he need never doubt his parents' affection for him. He will have to work to earn the affection and acceptance of others and in some cases he will fail, but through it all he can feel that he is not completely left out.

Being an effective parent means being able to enforce requirements and restrictions without arousing antagonism in the child. It means managing the routine demands on the child without arousing resentment. This can be accomplished only when these requirements are made impersonal and are clearly not just the whims of the parent. Thus the child is helped to realize that he goes to bed, or washes his hands, or does any of the other routine daily activities not because the parent wants these things done but because they are necessary parts of the business of living.

Another important feature of the parent-child relationship is mutual confidence and trust, that is, the parent trusts the child and the child trusts the parent. Any suspicion of each other causes the parent-child relationship to suffer. The parent can earn the child's confidence and trust by being completely reliable, that is by never deliberately deceiving the child. Some parents seem to think that deceit is justified if they succeed in getting the child to conform, but they fail to realize that the child loses faith in them. It is necessary also that the parents keep faith with the child by giving truthful answers to his questions, especially those difficult questions about sex. Keeping promises is another must. It is much better never to make promises to the child than to promise often and fail often to deliver. Promises carelessly made and not fulfilled tend to undermine the child's trust in the parent and it is impossible to have a happy and effective parent-child relationship without this trust.

It is equally important that the parent show trust and confidence in the child. This is even more difficult because the child in his immaturity is often unreliable. He may tell lies as most children do, or pilfer, or fail to live up to some of his responsibilities, but none of these shortcomings should cause the parent to lose faith in the child. It is this faith that helps the child to achieve slowly and gradually greater dependability. One father on discovering a series of examples of pilfering by his young son said that he could never trust him again. This father failed to realize that his lack of faith in his son would make it more difficult for the boy to learn more desirable forms of behaviour.

Sometimes the parents' lack of faith in their children leads them to check up too closely on them and to require them to account for every moment of their time. Thus the child in order to have any feeling of individual freedom, is forced to resort to deceit. Constant checking and too rigid supervision lead to resentment and sometimes even rebellion with consequent damage to the parent-child relationship. Children need some privacy and even secrets from their parents. Parents need to respect the possessions and private affairs of their children. One child complained that his mail was opened and that he didn't even have a bureau drawer or pants pocket that he could call his own.

Because so many of the parents' contacts with the child are for purposes of enforcing requirements and directing his behaviour, it is essential that there be occasions when the parent and child have happy times together. Some children have really fine people for parents but they have never found it out because about the only contact they have with them is when they are being disciplined. In order to build up or sustain a happy parent-child relationship there must be frequent occasions when parent and child engage in pleasant, friendly and happy activities together.

When things go wrong between parent and child, as they occasionally do, it is the parents' responsibility to try to mend the breach. It is so easy for little misunderstandings and resentments to grow that the sooner such things are cleared up the better. Sometimes the simplest way to manage this is to have a regular family council when every member of the family, young and old, has an opportunity to get things off his chest. Human relationships are complex and, since it is so easy for things to go wrong, it is desirable to have an easy and frequent way of clearing up difficulties. Parents sometimes need to listen and through listening to discover what generates resentment. Free discussion often helps to clear up misunderstandings. Such free discussion is not easy to manage because of the parental tendency to lay down the law and insist that father or mother knows best.

Sometimes parent-child relationships are helped by "heart-to-heart" talks between one parent and one child. This should not be spoiled by another parental habit of moralizing. In such private conferences parent and child can get closer to each other and often remove barriers of misunderstanding. Sometimes the boy or girl "opens up" and reveals thoughts, feelings and ambitions or doubts, fears and confusions which the parent would never have known about otherwise. Such confidential talks are difficult to arrange. It is almost impossible to plan them ahead of time, but the alert parent is ready to grasp the occasion when it presents itself.

There are some children who feel smothered by parental affection when it keeps them from becoming more and more independent as they grow up. The child can learn to depend less and less on the parent for care and direction and at the same time retain and even strengthen his affection for the parent. The parent-child relationship can become even more meaningful as the child grows away from the detailed supervision which was necessary in the early years of his life. When he is more "on his own" he can be even more than before on a basis of friendship with the parent. Part of the business of parenthood is the ability to become gradually less of a parent and more of a friend.

By way of summary we make the following practical suggestions:

1 Parents can and should enjoy their children; in fact, enjoyment of contacts with children is one of the best tests of effective parenthood.
2 Affection should never be used as a method of control.
3 Requirements and restrictions should be impersonal, required by the situation and not by a parental whim.
4 Trust and mutual confidence between parent and child can be maintained by complete parental reliability and an abiding trust in the child.
5 A too constant check-up on the child is undesirable.
6 Frequent happy times together help to maintain a healthy parent-child relationship.
7 Occasions can be found for confidential personal chats between parent and child.
8 Affection should not hinder the child's progress towards independence.

Chapter 4

The School

THE SECOND GREAT INFLUENCE on the child's development is the school. How can the school and the home best be co-ordinated in order to maximize the benefit to the child? What should the role of the parent be with respect to homework? How far should the child go in the educational system? These are some of the questions discussed in the articles in this chapter.

The home and school[1]

Home and school – two great institutions with the same goal. Both are trying to achieve the same end – the production of happy, well-adjusted adults. There should be no conflict between home and school, and for the good of the children there must be none. One of our pressing problems, however, is how to achieve the kind of co-operation between home and school which will best serve their common purpose.

It is most important that parents and teachers know and understand each other. Teachers give the impression that the home is falling down on the job, whereas many parents are highly critical of what the school is doing. It becomes obvious that these two groups of people need to get to know each other better and to understand each other's problems. In the old-fashioned rural school the teacher was a member of the community, known to all the parents and in turn well acquainted with all the parents as individuals. He often lived in a number of the homes, sharing the chores and the everyday problems of family life. But today, in the cities and towns and even in some rural communities, the teacher is relatively a stranger and knows nothing about the families and family life of the boys and girls he teaches. So one of our problems is to invent ways and means for the teacher and parents to get to know each other better.

One very common complaint of teachers is that children are sent off to school with inadequate preparation for the experience. Here is a place where greater co-operation between home and school is possible. Perhaps it isn't going too far to say that such co-operation should begin at the child's birth. The importance of the first five years of the child's life has been emphasized many times. Most parents and teachers accept this fact, but many parents need help and advice so that the training

1   K. S. Bernhardt, "The home and school," *Bull. Inst. Child Stud.*, 1953, 16 (3), 1 – 4.

and management of the child in these early years will help the child to adjust to the school experience.

Some schools have compiled suggestions designed to help parents prepare their children for school. It is difficult to include all of the things a child should have learned before he is ready for school, but the following list is at least suggestive. The child who has made progress in most of these will have a much easier and happier time when he starts on the great adventure of formal education:

He has learned to attend to his own toilet needs without supervision.
He can wash his own hands and face.
He can eat and drink with some skill and without assistance.
He can dress and undress himself without assistance – with a few exceptions such as snow suits and shoe laces.
He can manage the traffic situation; he can cross streets and knows when and where to do so.
He has acquired the necessary caution in handling sharp instruments, matches, and other potentially dangerous objects.
He has acquired the ability to manipulate materials and make simple constructions.
He is familiar with common objects in his environment and knows their names.
He has acquired a fair degree of control of the large muscles – running, jumping, climbing, etc.
He can understand simple directions and carry them out.
He has learned to accept necessary restrictions and rules.
He talks clearly and readily with no "baby talk."
He is content without his parents – goes places without them, stays home when they are not there.
He can amuse himself – has some initiative and self-sufficiency.
He has discarded temper tantrums as a method of getting his desires.
He has no serious and disturbing fears. He feels fairly secure and "at home."
He does not sulk or whine, but has learned to accept the consequences of his behaviour.
Tears are infrequent, not the usual response to any little discomfort or disappointment.
He has learned to play with other children without too much conflict or quarrelling.
He welcomes new experiences and chances to experiment and explore.
He knows the meaning of ownership of possessions.

This seems like a long list, but it could be even longer. It appears to be a lot for the young child to have learned in those few short years, and it is. However, it is not impossible and is certainly desirable. Leaving the comparatively sheltered world of the home for the broader world of the school can mean a difficult adjustment, but if the child is prepared for it there should be little difficulty. It is easy for parents to shelter and protect the child so much in the pre-school years that he is ill prepared for school. Emancipation of the child from his parents is a process which should begin early. Before he starts to school he can be encouraged to do many things for himself and to become independent of help and protection in the simpler things of everyday living.

When the child starts to school there are many more opportunities for active co-operation between home and school. One of these is the sharing of knowledge about the child. This can and should be a two-way process.

In order that the school may do a good job with the child, the teachers must have accurate information about his health, emotional adjustments, interests, special abilities, and defects. This must be provided in such a way that the teacher does not feel that the parent is asking for special treatment of his child but rather that he is sharing information pertinent for better understanding and treatment of him. Some schools welcome this kind of information, others do not. It is desirable for the school to have devised some routine and easy way of gathering such information and at the same time of getting a fairly clear picture of the kind of home the child comes from and the kind of parents he has.

But sharing information works in the other direction too – from the school to the home. The traditional report card seems a very slight and inadequate contribution to this information. No report card, however complete it may be, can do the whole job. Personal contact is necessary. Parent's Night at school once a year, although a step in the right direction, also seems inadequate. Some method is required which provides the necessary time for the teacher to discuss with the child's parents the total picture of the child's development. Mutual confidence and trust must be established so that when the school locates tooth, eye, nutritional, or intellectual defects the parents are ready to accept the information and do their share to effect a remedy.

Co-operation between home and school is also essential in the matter of the number and variety of special activities the child engages in. Many parents in their ambition for their children tend to fill the day with so many kinds of special lessons (music, dancing, swimming, etc.) that not only is there a real danger of fatigue and overstrain but no time for free play as well. The parent should know what the school demands in the way of work and extracurricular activities, and should make a real attempt to fit in only those things which do not overload the child.

Parents and teachers can co-operate more fully in character, sex, and religious education. Many parents today seem to expect the school to do their work for them in these areas. The school can supplement the home in sex education, but the home has a responsibility in this area as well. Character is, of course, the product of all the experiences the child has had, and the home cannot expect the school to remedy its deficiencies. Religious education can also be a co-operative venture, but here again the home must retain the major responsibility. Because the school has expanded its aims from a narrow intellectual development to the broader aspects of personality and character development does not mean that the home can lessen its efforts. There is a place for home and school discussion and co-operation in all these aspects of the child's development.

The Home and School Association can be a very effective and useful organization for co-operation between home and school. There are, however, three main dangers which should be kept in mind. (1) The Home and School Association may degenerate into a mere social club and neglect its main function of bringing about more effective working co-operation. (2) The Association can become a mere money-raising institution for school purposes which might better be taken care of by public funds. (3) Parents may think that the contact with the school through its organization is all that is needed and consequently neglect the more intimate contacts with school and teacher which are so essential for vital co-operation. These are not imaginary dangers for they can be observed in many associations.

To summarize we present some of the highlights of home and school co-operation.

WHAT THE SCHOOLS CAN DO

1 Acquaint parents with the ideals, goals, and methods of the school. Most schools have neglected this necessary public-relations job so far.

2 Find out about the home setting of the child. This provides a basis for many decisions in dealing with him.

3 Stimulate study of mutual problems by parent-teacher groups. Many problems which otherwise might hinder the effective guidance of the child in both home and school can be solved in this way.

4 Encourage friendly informal visits of parents while the school is in session.

5 Have frequent "open house" events so that parents see the products and progress of the children in the school and understand better what the school is trying to do.

6 Keep parents informed about the progress of the child in both his school work and his general development. This cannot be taken care of adequately by a formal school report but requires face-to-face informal discussion.

WHAT PARENTS CAN DO

1 Make it their business to know what the school is doing, what its goals and methods are. Many parents today think of the schools as being the same as when they were children, whereas most schools have changed considerably in the last two decades. Parents should be interested in and informed about these changes.

2 Take an intelligent interest in school policies, methods, financing, and selection of teachers, that is, know what the school board is doing and why.

3 Do not spoil the child's attitude towards school and teachers by criticizing them in the hearing of children.

4 Provide the school with abundant information about the child.

5 Get to know the child's teachers. Initiate friendly contacts.

6 Do not expect the school to assume the whole responsibility for the education of the child. There are many areas of education in which the home has the major responsibility, for example, manners, morals, religion, health habits, and play.

The school and mental health[2]

It is our belief that a school setting that will help to build a solid foundation for mental health can be fashioned. We believe also that the school-age period is crucial in establishing the mental health of the individual for life. The child's experiences during this period will determine to a large extent the nature of his general adjustment to life and thus the level of his mental health.

We are not suggesting that the school is the only setting or even the most important in the building of these foundations. The home undoubtedly takes first place, but the school follows it very closely in importance. What the school experiences will mean to the child will depend to a great extent on the nature of the home relationships. However, while recognizing the prior importance of the home and family relationships, we wish to focus our attention on the role of the school in the mental health development of children.

It is our contention that going to school can be a happy, profitable

2 K. S. Bernhardt, "The school and mental health," *Bull. Inst. Child Stud.*, 1963, 25 (4), 1 - 4.

experience for all children. It is our observation that this is not true for all children; there are many who find school a strain and a burden, with experiences that are detrimental to their health and well-being. In the following paragraphs we shall try to identify various school conditions and methods, relate them to the development of the child, and evaluate their effect on his mental health.

The school was organized as a way of providing help for parents in guiding the learning of their children when they discovered they did not have the time and competence to do the whole job. Gradually a set of ideas evolved about what should be taught (curriculum) and how it should be taught (methods). The effectiveness of the process was judged mainly in terms of speed of learning and accuracy of performance. It is only recently that other criteria have been employed in evaluation.

We now ask more than what was learned and how fast. We want to know what effect the learning has had on the developing character and personality of the child. As has been said many times, "the whole child goes to school." So in every situation where the child is being supervised we have a dual purpose: to take care of the immediate situation guiding the child so that his behaviour is adequate and fitting and at the same time to be concerned about the long-range effects of the experience on the character and personality of the child. For instance, when we think only of the immediate results, the easiest and most successful method of getting the child to behave in a certain way is bribery. The child will do almost anything within his present ability if we make the bribe attractive enough. When, however, we look beyond the immediate results to what the child is becoming we doubt whether it is a good method after all.

In thinking about mental health and the school we usually think of the provision of people and facilities to deal with problem behaviour, maladjustment, and academic failures. But this is only a programme of mental health and does not play as important a part as efforts to ensure that the methods and everyday routines of the school are conducive to good mental health. We recognize the value of child adjustment services and programmes of re-education and therapy, but we feel that efforts to eliminate those methods and conditions which make the adjustment services necessary are much more valuable.

When we look at developmental material we see that in the early years of the school-age period the child is building a self-picture. The nature of this self-picture is basic to his mental health. The child needs to feel that he is a worthy individual. He needs to see himself as capable. He must have sufficient self-confidence to meet and cope with the demands of his environment.

The school often makes it difficult for the child to build this necessary self-confidence. The use of marks, standing, ranking, passing, and failing allows only a few in the group to feel adequate. A high value is placed on academic success, but when success is evaluated in terms of doing something better or faster than everyone else only a minority of the group can qualify, the rest are forced to use distortion or defence mechanism to compensate for their lack of success.

The deliberate use of competition in school work should be discarded, but how can we motivate children to learn without using some aspect of competition? An answer to this question leads us to the distinction between extrinsic and intrinsic motivation and our contention that intrinsic is better than extrinsic motivation. By intrinsic motivation we mean features of the learning activity itself; extrinsic motivation indicates the addition of other features. Extrinsic incentives include prizes, rewards and awards, honour rolls, and notations of standing. Intrinsic incentives include feelings of achievement and progress and of adequacy. Most learning carries its own intrinsic motivation and does not require the extrinsic incentives added by the schools. The school would be more mentally healthy if artificial incentives, comparisons between children, and other discouraging features were eliminated.

I am not suggesting that everything be made easy for the child, but I am implying that the child must have faith in himself and a feeling of adequacy if he is to be mentally healthy. When he has recurring experiences of failure in his school work it is very difficult for him to maintain adequate self-confidence. One of the most important functions of the teacher is to provide re-assurance, support, and encouragement for the child.

Much of the usual routine of adult supervision of children is negative and corrective, whereas what the child needs is positive direction that is supportive and encouraging. Much of the deviant behaviour in children stems from experiences in which the child has been made to feel inadequate. Lacking a feeling of self-worth he compensates in immature ways and this in turn reduces his chances of feeling adequate.

Time and again teachers have seen improvement in a child's behaviour following a change in treatment from discouragement to encouragement. Sometimes improvement follows some casual remark which expresses the teacher's faith in the child. The child seems to need to feel that someone believes in him before he can believe in himself.

The most important aspect of a mentally healthy environment for development is the presence of an adult (parent, teacher, leader) who is capable of providing support, reassurance, and encouragement to the children. It is clear then that teachers should be adequately prepared for their job. Whether one year at Teachers' College after graduation from High School is sufficient preparation for the exacting job of guiding the development of a group of children is doubtful. Certainly "sufficient preparation" would include an understanding of the importance of reassurance, support, and encouragement, and also of how detrimental criticism and belittling can be.

We can look at the various methods and procedures used in the school in much the same way, trying to assess the effect they have on the mental health of the children. We find that some methods in common use are detrimental to healthy development. By way of summary we shall list some of these detrimental methods and conditions and also some that are helpful.

METHODS AND CONDITIONS DETRIMENTAL
TO MENTAL HEALTH

1 Anything that makes it difficult for the child to build and maintain self-confidence.

2 Inconsistent discipline which makes it difficult for the child to know what is expected of him.

3 Learning tasks beyond the child's present ability.

4 Failure to take into account the individual differences in ability, interests, and stage of development.

5 An emphasis on marks, standing, and passing or failing.

6 The use of artificial incentives.

7 The deliberate use of competition in school work.

8 The use of pain and fear of pain as a method of control.

9 A strict authoritarian kind of control with no allowance for individual choice and decision.

10 Rote learning or memory work with little or no understanding of material.

CONDITIONS AND METHODS THAT AID
MENTAL HEALTH

1 Thorough acceptance of the child as he is so that he will feel wanted and at home in the school.

2 The adjustment of the level of difficulty of material to the present level of ability of the child so that his learning tasks are neither too difficult nor too easy.

3 A flexible curriculum so that individual differences in ability and interest can be taken into account.

4 Some freedom of choice and practice in self-direction so that not all school activities are imposed and teacher-directed.

5 The arranging of learning situations so that there will be a maximum of discovery and a minimum of drill and rote learning.

6 Discipline that is consistent and reasonable and non-punitive.

7 Teachers who understand children and who are aware of the importance of the child's self-picture and his need of reassurance and encouragement.

8 Co-operation of parents and teachers and adequate exchange of information about the child.

9 Prompt dealing with deviant behaviour so that "problem behaviour" does not become too acute.

10 Selection of curriculum material so that it is as close as possible to the interests and curiosities of the children.

Homework – parental worry or opportunity?[3]

All parents like to see their children do well at school. Many parents are so concerned about the child's school progress that they will go to almost any length to see that he succeeds. To some parents this means checking up constantly and minutely on the child's homework to make sure that it is done and done perfectly. They take the responsibility for seeing that it is done even if on occasion this means doing it themselves. Sometimes this results in a battle royal, tears, and unpleasantness. To these parents homework is a worry.

To some other parents the child's homework is an opportunity, a chance to show an interest in what the child is learning, to participate in the adventure of discovery. These parents welcome the chance to stimulate and encourage, to help the child find information, to guide

3 K. S. Bernhardt, "Homework – parental worry or opportunity?" Inst. Child Study Pamphlet, no. 7, pp. 2 – 5.

the development of habits of interest, concentration, and efficiency. Homework to them is not a worry, it is an opportunity.

First, let us ask and try to answer the question "what is the function of homework?" Many people have been saying recently that homework is unnecessary, that there should be enough time in the school hours for school work and that the child should not be expected to continue it outside. Formal homework has been or is being abolished in the first few grades of school, and the suggestion is being made that it might be abolished in the upper grades as well. However, there is a very useful place for homework even in the early grades. Some of the reasons for it are the following: it is one method of dealing with the child who is slower than the average in his class – he can make up the work at home that he doesn't get finished at school. It is a way of getting some of the routine work done, thus leaving the school more time for the more interesting features of the curriculum. It is useful as a means of enriching the subject matter by tapping outside sources of information. It is one method of keeping the parents informed about the learning progress of the child.

It should be said that there is a great need for the school and the home to co-operate more closely on this matter of homework. The school should be more aware of those activities of children which are just as valuable and sometimes more valuable than homework and which are crowded out by it. Also, the school must take more responsibility in making known to the parents the reason for the homework, its kind and amount and how much time the child is expected to spend on it. On the other hand, the home (that is, the parents) should use every opportunity to find out about the school curriculum and how the home can help the child to acquire the skills and knowledge demanded. Homework is undoubtedly one area in which there could be more co-operation between home and school – two institutions with a common goal.

The child's homework is *his* responsibility, not the parents'. But this does not mean that the parents can not and should not take an interest in it. The desirable situation is, of course, that in which the child assumes the entire responsibility for getting his work done, for getting it done at the most convenient time, and for getting it done on time. The parent, however, has some responsibilities in this connection. One of these is the arrangement of the child's schedule of activities so that there *is* a convenient and acceptable time for homework. This should be done with the child's co-operation and he should be guided to construct a time schedule in which he plans his time and carries out the schedule as planned. The work itself, important as it is, is not nearly as important as the habits of work acquired in doing it. One very important habit that can be acquired in the homework situation is that of planning work and carrying through the plans. In this way the child acquires the habit of working while he works, that is, he concentrates on the task at hand and puts enough effort into it to carry it through to a successful completion.

Another parental responsibility in the homework situation is the arrangement of suitable work conditions. In order to get work done as well as for the more important consideration, learning to work, it is essential that a quiet place, in which the materials of work are at hand and in which distractions of all kinds are reduced to a minimum, be available. It is difficult, if not impossible, for the child to learn to work well in a room where a radio or television is blaring, or the rest of the family is carrying on conversation or other activities. It is also important that there be as few interruptions as possible, that the rest of the family respect the work times of the student and leave him to it. Since fear of interruption is almost as bad as actual interruption, it is essential for the child to feel confident that he will be undisturbed during his scheduled work periods.

It is also the responsibility of the parent to take an interest in the child's work. This does not mean that it is necessary to check up constantly but rather to give the child the assurance that you are available and interested. There should be less nagging and scolding and more recognition of his accomplishment. He doesn't feel then that he is being pushed by an ambitious parent but rather that he has a parent who is more interested in what he does than in whether he stands first in his class. Interest is infectious. The parent who is curious about what makes the wheels go round, who is still interested in learning new things, usually has children with a zeal for knowledge. Homework in such an atmosphere is not drudgery but a voyage of discovery.

One of the most important phases of the parent's part in homework is the arranging of ways and means for the child to have access to sources of information. This includes providing books of reference in some way or other. Governments have long lists of valuable pamphlets on many subjects related to the projects carried on in the schools today. Such source material can be obtained free or for a nominal amount. Most communities have public libraries with shelves full of reference books. In some cases this means that the parents have to arrange time and give guidance to the child in how to find and use these sources of information. The periodicals that come into the home can be made to serve this very useful purpose as well. The list of periodicals to which the family subscribes may need revision in order to provide the necessary source material. Putting the child in touch with adult friends who may be a fertile source of useful information can also be helpful.

How much help should the parent give the child? This is a very difficult question to answer. There are, however, a number of guiding principles that may be of assistance. Remember that the important thing is that the child should become increasingly capable of carrying on without assistance, increasingly responsible for his own work. There is nothing quite so pathetic as the student who has become so accustomed to having someone tell him exactly what to do, how and when to do it that when he is thrown on his own at university he is completely lost and doesn't get anything done. Good work habits and responsibility for carrying through tasks do not just happen. They are built up gradually and require considerable guidance along the way. One answer, then, to the above question is "just enough help to get the child over the more critical places" – help that is designed to assist the child learn where to find the information he needs, help that will enable him to keep his interest and curiosity very much alive. It is not real help to do the work for the child, dig out the answers for him, solve his problems, but rather a hindrance to the kind of learning we would like to see happen. I have heard of mothers who have gathered the material for some project, arranged it, and even in some cases put it together in a beautiful scrap book which the child took to school and exhibited as his own work. If the parent is to give help, it must be help, not the work itself.

A very important and often essential part of the parent's guidance of the child's homework is helping him to apportion his time so that no phase of his work is neglected. This does not mean that the child should not be allowed occasional splurges in some interesting subject matter, but it does mean that such a lack of balance among subjects should be infrequent. The child is very much like his parents, that is, he usually does first those things he can do best and in which he has the most interest, leaving to the last the more difficult tasks which at the same time are not as intrinsically interesting. He can be guided to change the order, to get the more difficult and less interesting things done first when he is fresher and has more energy available. He can be helped to concentrate on his weak spots. It is in these weaker subjects that he often requires the most help and guidance.

There are some kinds of homework that can be done best with other students and still other kinds that are hindered in the social study situation. You can help the child to judge what can be done best as a co-operative activity and what can be more effectively accomplished alone. One thing to remember is that group homework has its own values, and important ones they are too, but that it usually involves considerable wasted time as well. A simple method of dealing with this situation is to set a reasonable time limit on social homework, not allowing it to become too frequent. One of homework's greatest values is the opportunity it affords for individual planning, effort, and accomplishment.

The management of the details of homework must be a matter for each parent to decide in terms of his own particular circumstances – home conditions, number of other activities, amount of homework demanded by the school, and progress of the child. The guiding principles to be applied according to the individual situation are as follows:

1 Close co-operation between home and school in terms of objectives and curriculum.

2 Homework should be predominantly the child's own responsibility and whatever the parent does should be done with this in mind.

3 The methods of work, the habits of work acquired, and the attitudes toward work are more important than merely getting the work done.

4 It is the responsibility of the parents to provide good work conditions, with materials available, interruptions reduced to a minimum, and fear of interruptions banished.

5 The child should be helped to plan and schedule his work and to follow his plans.

6 Help should be given at the critical points, but not to the point where the work is done for the child.

7 Sources of information should be made available to the child and help in how to find information given.

8 Homework should not be a worry to the parent but an opportunity to keep in touch with the child's academic progress, to stimulate where necessary, to guide occasionally, and to help the child acquire independence and responsibility in work situations.

Choosing a career[4]

The choice of a vocation is one of the most important decisions that a boy or girl has to make. This is a decision that the individual should

4 K. S. Bernhardt, "Vocational guidance – advantages and changes," *Parent Educ. Bull.*, 1944, no. 30, 7 – 9.

make for himself. There is, however, no reason why he should not have some help with it. This is the function of vocational guidance – to provide the information the boy or girl needs to make a wise choice of his or her life work.

Vocational guidance in some form or other is not new. Parents have influenced or tried to influence their children in the choice of their vocations for years. However, the introduction of vocational guidance into the school system is a fairly recent development. It is desirable, therefore, that parents and teachers be informed as to what a programme of vocational guidance can do, how it might be carried on, and what the results might be.

A vocational guidance programme has certain obvious advantages. There are also distinct dangers. We shall look at these in turn. The advantages of the programme are, first, the provision of a fund of vocational information so that the student may learn what vocations there are and what each is like. A second advantage is the provision of facilities for the appraisal of the individual in terms of abilities, temperament, and interests, for example, thus providing him with a sounder basis for his choice. A third advantage of such a programme is that it brings clearly before the boy or girl the necessity of making this decision early enough so that his academic career will be a suitable preparation for the work he is to do later. The frequency of unwise vocational choices, the rather haphazard selection of work which later turns out to be unsatisfactory for the individual, and the worry and indecision of many young people all make some form of vocational guidance essential.

All that passes for vocational guidance, however, is not necessarily sound. The use of tests of various kinds by people who are not trained in their interpretation and limitations is a rather dangerous procedure. The attempt to steer an individual into a particular vocation, telling a boy that he should be a doctor or engineer or butcher without reliable information as to his suitability for the work, can be worse than no guidance at all. The task of directing a person into a line of work is too serious to be done in a haphazard manner. Many a boy or girl has received poor direction from an over-enthusiastic teacher who tells him that because he gets good marks in mathematics at High School he should take a particular course at university and prepare for a particular career. There is a misconception about vocational guidance which should be mentioned, that is that there is one job for which an individual is perfectly fitted and that the job of vocational guidance is merely to discover that perfect job by the magic of tests and other procedures. It should be stated definitely that people and jobs are not thus constituted – jobs and people do not fit. There is not one perfect job for anybody. There are, however, for any person some vocations that are more suitable than others, not just one job but a whole list of them in which he could probably succeed. The task of the vocational guidance person is, therefore, to help the individual discover what vocations offer for him the greater chance of success and what vocations are less likely to be suitable and then to let him make his own decision.

Now, to look at some of the details of a sound vocational guidance programme. Such a programme has two main phases: first, vocational education, and, second, guidance proper. A programme of vocational education should be designed to provide information about the kinds of work that are done in the world. This should begin very early in the educational programme, in the primary grades, and should include both first- and second-hand experience of a great variety of kinds of work. This programme can be and probably should be a co-operative venture in which the home, the school, and other community agencies take part. The important thing is that every boy and girl become familiar not with just one or two occupations but with a large number in terms of the work actually done and their place in the larger picture of human living.

The guidance phase of the total programme has two important parts – the appraisal of the individual and the knowledge of the requirements of various kinds of vocations. The appraisal of the individual should be fairly extensive and must be done in such a way that reliable information is obtained. In such an appraisal, the following aspects of the individual's make-up should be considered: (a) general ability – probably best evaluated by a reliable intelligence test administered by a person trained in the use of such tests; (b) an indication of various special abilities or aptitudes, such as mechanical, musical, artistic, clerical, which the individual may possess; again the easiest and most reliable method of obtaining this information is by means of tests, although a history of what the individual has done and how well he has done it also helps; (c) a summary of the individual's personality, including some indication of his general temperamental make-up, his attitudes, social skills, sense of values; (d) a picture of his interests; (e) information about the types of satisfaction he wants – financial, social, economic; (f) a picture of the individual's present educational attainments and the possibilities for further training.

In order to make use of the information obtained in an individual appraisal it is necessary to know the actual requirements of various vocations. This information should fit in with the factors outlined above. We should know: (a) what level of general ability is required by the various positions; (b) what special abilities and aptitudes are required; (c) what personality characteristics are important for success in the various vocations; (d) what interests are required; (e) the satisfactions provided by the various occupations, for example, salary scales, social position, etc.; (f) what educational standards and special courses are needed. Guidance then resolves itself into relating these two sets of information and trying to find the areas of work in which there is the best fit. This rarely indicates just one particular vocation but rather a number of them. At this stage such secondary considerations as the feasibility of getting the necessary training, the vocational opportunities at present available or likely to be available in the near future, and the individual's incidental preferences help to swing the decision in one or other direction.

Parents have been advised on occasion to keep out of this field, but this is not as good advice as that which indicates how parents can be of help. There is no doubt that parents can be of distinct help to their children in the matter of vocational choice, provided only that the help given by the parents does not take the form of making up the child's mind for him. Many examples could be quoted of parents deciding that their boy should be a doctor or minister or what-not and then bringing all the weight of their prestige and influence to bear on him until there seems no other course open to him but the road mapped out by his parents. In a few cases this works out well, but in a great many other cases it ends in disaster. Parents can, nevertheless, be helpful in a number of ways – providing opportunities for the child to find out about various lines of work, discussing in an objective way the various possibilities, being sympathetic and understanding about the indecision of the child, and putting the boy or girl in touch with those who are equipped to offer sound vocational advice. Finally, perhaps the way in which parents can help most is by keeping a close check on their inevitable ambitions for the child which may be unrealistic or impracticable.

Who should go to college?[5]

Although every year there is increasing pressure for individuals to receive a college education, it is quite evident that everyone cannot and

5   D. K. Bernhardt, "Who should go to college?" Revision of article by K. S. Bernhardt in *Can. School J.*, October 1936.

should not go to college. Therefore, despite the fact that this extremely important question has never been answered satisfactorily, some kind of answer is required for the individuals facing the problem and for the parents and guidance teachers who must face it with them. Let us look at some of the guiding principles.

In the first place the colleges themselves lay down certain requirements for entrance. These requirements vary slightly from one university to another but they do rule out a good many individuals who are not able to meet them. Another important selecting factor is money. To many individuals this is still an almost insurmountable obstacle even though colleges and governments are doing a great deal to provide financial assistance for needy but deserving students.

Should all those students who can meet the entrance requirements and find the money go to college? It seems fairly obvious that the individuals who should go to college are those who can profit from the experience. But how can we best determine those students who can profit most from a college career? The standard of university success as set down by university authorities is examination results. It is true that this is not a good standard. Certainly most students who fail on examinations still profit by this university experience but it may be that their time and effort could have been more profitably spent elsewhere.

In many colleges, at least one out of every three students fails in his first year. This is, of course, a highly selected group of students, but even so there is a significant relationship between success in high school and success in college. Therefore a student whose high school record places him near the lower end of the distribution of high school students has a very slight chance of being successful in university work. Here then is one basis for the selection of students who should or should not enter university.

Younger students tend to do better than older students at university. Of course, there are other factors involved here. The students who are older when they enter college may have advanced through public and high schools at a slower rate thus suggesting lower than average ability. On the other hand these students may have spent a number of years out of school working and experience difficulty returning to academic work. Both of these factors, however, tend to militate against successful university work.

Today we are seeing more and more students who clearly have the ability to succeed at college but who, nevertheless, are failing to pass or are dropping out. The majority of these students are not interested in their college work and are unwilling to put the required effort into it. Pressure to go to college has been placed on them at home or at school, but they are not ready for the experience. In such cases they would be better advised to wait for a year or two until they are ready to meet the challenge.

It is impossible to really answer the question of who should go to college, but we offer some suggestions here. In the first place, it is evident that one very important factor in university success is high school performance. There are a number of other factors related to readiness for college – motivation and interests, emotional stability, and ability to adjust to new situations. Such factors as study methods and reading skill will influence the student's chances for success.

Chapter 5

Development Through the Years

EACH STAGE OF DEVELOPMENT has its own special problems. It is important for all parents to understand the different problems associated with the advances of the child towards maturity. In the articles in this chapter attention is successively focused on the first five years of life, the first years of school, and the adolescent years.

The first five years[1]

It has been said many times that the first five years of an individual's life are the most important because what happens then determines to a great extent what may happen later on. Whether this is true or not it is certainly true that these years cannot be overlooked in any attempt to account for the personality of the adult. It is also true that all stages in the development of the individual are important and that there is a definite relationship between what takes place at one stage of development and what takes place at all later stages.

The best guarantee of successful adjustment at any stage of development is the individual's satisfactory adjustment at all previous stages of development. In order to illustrate this basic principle and to bring out the importance of the first five years let us begin by looking at a development scheme based on the individual's adjustment to his ever-changing environment.

The first development period is usually called infancy. This is the period of comparative helplessness. The child at birth is immature, almost completely helpless, and dependent on someone else's care. He knows nothing and can do very little, but he is capable of learning and starts this process almost immediately. What he learns now forms the foundation for subsequent learning. His needs as a human being form the basis for his learning. Very early he learns that other people are important to him. He becomes aware of the fact that whenever his needs are satisfied some other person is involved. He soon learns also that his own behaviour has its effect in that when he cries, for instance, someone gives him attention. He may learn to get what he wants by crying or he may learn that food and attention come at regular times irrespective of his howls. But whatever it is he learns, the inevitable thing is that he does learn something, and the important thing is that he should learn what will help him in further development.

1 K. S. Bernhardt, "The first five years," *Parent. Educ. Bull.*, 1943, no. 24, 2 – 6.

This first period of helpless infancy comes to an end when he is able to walk. Now instead of being a cute little ornament which stays put in a crib or a playpen he has become a person who moves about in his world and can get into trouble, who must learn that there are things he cannot do and that there are things he must do. He is now a pre-school child. This is a period of rapid and important learning. The sooner this child learns that there are two very different kinds of activities, the better, those things he must do whether he wants to or not and those things he can do or not as he likes. The first are usually called routines and the second play. Because of his rapid physical growth and maturation his almost continual activity during his waking moments, the child quickly acquires better and better muscular co-ordination and learns to do more and more things. Other people in his world are becoming increasingly important to him. He has started to learn what it means to live in a social world. The more of the right kinds of learning he absorbs during this period the better he will be equipped for later periods of adjustment. We shall look at this picture in more detail later.

The pre-school period comes to an end when the child starts to school at the age of five or six. Now he leaves the comparatively sheltered home environment for a part of the day and becomes a member of a much wider social group. He encounters a new type of discipline, many new adjustments, and much to learn. Adjustment in this period is sometimes very difficult to make since it depends upon what the child has already learned or failed to learn. If he has been helped to make a satisfactory adjustment during the pre-school period he will not find this new situation too difficult. However, if he has failed to adjust satisfactorily in the earlier period or if he has failed to learn some of the usual skills, both social and physical, he may have a very hard time fitting in with the new situation.

The next period – adolescence – begins when the maturing of the reproductive system takes place and the secondary sexual characteristics appear. This has been called a period of peculiar stress and strain, a period of difficult adjustment, but it need not be a time of particular difficulty, and is so only when the first ten or twelve years of life have not been well spent. The child who has been guided to learn and adjust happily to the various situations he meets does not as a rule have great problems of adjustment during adolescence. True, the adolescent usually finds himself in a state of mild conflict, wanting at the same time to be thought of as "grown-up" and to have the security of dependence on his parents.

Perhaps the most important stage in development is the achievement of the transition from child to adult, an all-round maturity, social and emotional as well as physical and intellectual. An adult is one who can make his own decisions, adjust satisfactorily in the social world, and "run his own life." This is the goal of all guidance and education from birth on, and this goal can be the basis for decisions about methods and techniques of handling the child all along the line. We can decide most questions of policy in child training by asking and finding the answer to the simple question: "What will help the child most to achieve self-discipline, independence, and maturity?"

Some of the major adjustments usually required in adolescence and adulthood should be mentioned here because they illustrate the principle introduced earlier that each succeeding stage of development builds on previous stages. One of these is the vocational adjustment of the individual. His ability to adjust to the world of work depends on the attitudes, the skills, and the knowledge he has acquired from infancy on. This is also true of such an important adjustment as what is usually called "falling in love." A person's adjustment to the opposite sex and to a particular member of the opposite sex depends directly on the kind of sex education he has had during his pre-school years. Recent investigations in marital success or failure have clearly indicated the importance of early experiences and types of training.

It is equally true that adjustments to parenthood and to middle and old age depend on what the individual has learned from his previous experiences and the degree of success he has achieved in dealing with them.

All stages of development, then, depend on all earlier stages. The importance of the first five years can be simply stated by saying that since they come first what happens then helps to determine what will happen later.

The forgotten years – six to twelve[2]

The pre-school years have received a good deal of attention and adolescence has always been interesting, but the intervening years are often

2　K. S. Bernhardt, "The forgotten years, 6 – 12," *Parent Educ. Bull.*, 1943, no. 25, 2 – 7.

neglected. This seems to be true of both research and training. We know more about the first five years than we do about the second five. Although parents seem to lose some of their enthusiasm for child training after the child's fifth birthday, the in-between years *are* important. The experiences of these years have a share in determining the course of adolescence and of later life.

WHAT IS THE SCHOOL-AGE CHILD LIKE?

The first essential in dealing with the child of this age as with every other age is understanding. Every experience is his own; his abilities, interests, attitudes, habits, weaknesses and needs are peculiarly his. He doesn't stand still, he is constantly changing – growing, developing, learning. There are, however, similarities and there are broad general principles that apply to all school-age children. It is these similarities and general principles that we shall try to develop in the following paragraphs.

Physical make-up
One of the most noticeable features of the school-age child is his abundant energy. He doesn't seem to be capable of sitting still for any length of time – he must be doing things. In any planning for this child then, it is necessary to keep in mind that he must have outlets for his abundant energy. A certain amount of noise and strenuous activity can be expected. The adult – parent or teacher – who expects or demands quiet orderly behaviour from the school-age child is merely manufacturing difficulties for himself. The child's rapid physical development also gives rise to problems of nutrition, health, exercise, and sleep. There is great danger here that too much concern on the part of the parent will place undue emphasis on these matters. The regularity of eating, sleeping, and other routines should be maintained and taken for granted in a matter-of-fact manner. Where there are individual differences in physique and rate of growth and development, it is easy for the parent to be concerned that the child is not as large as other children of his age, that his height or weight is not up to the average. This concern can generate fears in the child that there is something wrong with him or that he is inferior to other children and these fears may have far-reaching results in terms of the child's behaviour and emotional development. The child's increasing motor skills bring parental responsibility to provide materials and the time and place for learning new skills. The parent must allow an increasing scope for new activities.

Emotional behaviour

The school-age child should show increasing emotional control. The occasions when he loses control in a temper tantrum, for instance, should be less and less frequent. Normally crying as a mode of emotional expression decreases. Increasing ability to resist physical and social provocation, that is, to adjust in situations without emotional disturbance should be evident. Since the child is learning more about his world and is gaining more skill in handling practical situations, occasions for emotional disturbance should be fewer. The school-age child is more sensitive than the pre-school child to approval and disapproval. Since he is especially sensitive to ridicule both from adults and from other children, ridicule as a technique should be avoided. The child needs help in learning to adjust to the ridicule of the group. He needs to learn to evaluate ridicule and to acquire a balance between being too sensitive and not sensitive enough to what others think of him. Normally his fears will decrease in number and intensity, as he learns to adjust to new situations and to face potential fear situations and conquer them. Incidentally, the school-age child usually learns to dislike emotional displays of any kind. He does not like to have his parents make a fuss over him, especially in the presence of other children.

Social development

In the school-age period there is an increasing understanding of social requirements, manners, and customs. The child wants to know what is done and why. This desire should be met, not by formal instruction in manners but rather by informal discussions of manners and customs. Usually he wants to conform, but at the same time he doesn't want to be made to conform. His social world is expanding with contacts outside the home. He is learning loyalty to friends and companions. Sometimes this loyalty conflicts with his loyalty to his home and parents. Here, again, the school-age child needs help and understanding. Very frequently during this period there is a separation of the sexes. The interests and activities of boys and girls do, of course, differ, but there is a danger in making this separation too definite. Foolish adult attitudes with teasing and silly remarks which lead the child to thinking of companionship with the opposite sex as being unnatural and undesirable are also dangerous. It is desirable that contacts with the opposite sex be natural and frequent, so that the boy or girl will not have to start from the beginning when he or she reaches adolescence. Each should learn to understand and appreciate the opposite sex and enjoy contacts with them.

Interests

The interests of the school-age child tend to be more restricted and specialized than those of the pre-school child. This specialization is to be expected but, if the child has a wide variety of experiences and an opportunity for a wide variety of activities, the specialization will not be too rapid or too narrow. His activities tend to be more creative and dramatic or symbolic, and he shows a marked jump in persistence. Many parents worry about the activities of the school-age child. They think that he is wasting most of his time in useless activities. These parents often try to force interests on the child, but it is better that his interests be his own. He is often learning more from his seemingly useless and time-wasting activities than we realize. Of course, it is a good idea to provide the materials and equipment as well as the place and the time for the development of interests, but this sometimes means that the parent must be patient until the child "gets around" to making use of this material. Any attempt to force interests usually serves to kill them. The school-age child will be attracted by fads and fashions in activities, doing those things which other children are doing.

REGULATION OF THE SCHOOL-CHILD'S ACTIVITY

The close supervision and regulation of the child's activities which were necessary during the pre-school years become less and less so as the child grows older. Discipline and regulation during this time build on the foundation laid in the early years but are now exercised with more flexibility. The growing understanding of the child makes it increasingly possible to stress the reasonableness of the requirements and to enlist the child's co-operation in helping to make the rules. The objectives of the regulation are, of course, to guide the child to a greater self-discipline, to help him to learn to accept willingly the necessary regulations of living, to manage his own activities, and to learn how to get along well with other people.

The basis of regulation is a set of planned requirements. These basic requirements are decided by the parents who, of course, must continue to take the major responsibility for their administration. The authority of the parent should rest on prestige built up by consistent, friendly, and reasonable direction of the child and his environment. It is essential that the general pattern of the requirements be clearly reasonable. When the general picture is thus understood and accepted by the child, it is possible for him to accept some requirements that he cannot understand and whose value is not apparent to him. The parent and child should work together in deciding on the details of some of the requirements, and as the child grows older he should be given more and more opportunity to take part in the planning and administration. During the school-age period a certain degree of flexibility is desirable, that is, reasonable exceptions may be made when the activity which interferes with the routine requirements is more desirable than rigid adherence to the established routine. Since the requirements change with the development and learning of the child, a periodic examination and revision of requirements is called for. This revision is made on the basis of the child's demonstration of dependability and management of freedom.

There should be a clear distinction between required activities and free activities. The required activities are the routine and work activities of the school-age child. They include school work plus homework, other formal lessons such as music, swimming, home chores, care of possessions, and personal care. The child's daily programme should be planned thoughtfully so that the required activities are sufficiently balanced with free activities. The child of this age can take part in this planning. Decisions can be made jointly on when the homework is to be done, what extra lessons should be taken, what home duties he is to be responsible for, and when these chores are to be done. The parent must be ready and willing to extend responsibility to the child whenever there is any indication that he is ready for it. Parental standards of performance should not exceed either the child's ability or understanding of the task. Blame, scolding, and a feeling of martyrdom on the part of the parent are out of place in this situation. Discussion of his performance with the child is desirable but should take place at a time when there is no issue involved or requirement to be fulfilled. Argument, emotional scenes, and battles over the requirements are unnecessary and undesirable.

Minute regulation in the free activities is uncalled for. A certain amount of regulation is necessary in such aspects as geographical limits, time, and reasonable consideration for others, but this can be arranged without giving the child a feeling of being hemmed in or restricted. Freedom in play and leisure time activities is essential, and these activities must fit into a reasonable schedule. The child should learn that he can have his freedom within reasonable limits but that meal hours and bed-time hours are necessary.

The most effective force in the regulation of the child is the example and friendly companionship of the parent. Leadership gets better results than dictatorship. It is highly desirable that the child find in the parent affection and companionship. Much of importance that he learns during this period happens indirectly; he is absorbing the attitudes, manners, and moral standards of his world. This requires a relationship with his parents which is conducive to free discussion. He needs not a parent who will lay down the law and tell him what is right, but a parent who can talk things over with him and help him to see what is involved in situations so that he can make up his own mind and form his own opinions. Consequently in all our contacts with the school-age child it is well to keep in mind that we are trying to produce a self-regulated individual who can make his own decisions, who can weigh and evaluate issues, and who can effectively and happily run his own life.

Adolescents need understanding[3]

To many parents and teachers, adolescents are puzzles. The happy carefree boy or girl of a few short years ago is now an unpredictable enigma. Some parents, say, "He is just going through the adolescent stage," as though that explained everything. Parents of adolescents, however, need to do more than just "put up" with the adolescent; they need to try to understand him. This is all the more important because the adolescent does not usually understand himself, and he needs to feel that he has the sympathetic understanding of some adults – especially his own parents and some of his teachers.

The adolescent is often fundamentally insecure. This is because he faces a number of very serious problems for which he must find some solution. The problems which confront the adolescent are as important, serious, and far-reaching in their effects as any he will meet during his whole lifetime. First, he must decide about his vocational career. Second, both biological and social pressures drive him to an interest in the

3 K. S. Bernhardt, "Adolescents need understanding," *Bull. Inst. Child Stud.*, 1955, 17 (2) , 5 – 8.

opposite sex, and thus start the process which will likely culminate in the selection of a life partner. Third, he must learn to stand on his own feet, make his own decisions, and become a truly independent person; sometimes this emancipation from parental control is painful and difficult for both parent and adolescent. Finally, he is often faced with the problem of formulating a satisfying philosophy of life. Is it any wonder that he feels insecure?

The adolescent's insecurity is expressed in many ways, most of them puzzling and annoying to parents and teachers. He may be noisy and a show-off, or he may be quiet, self-conscious, and withdrawn. He may appear at times to be sulky and insolent. He may insist on wearing faddish clothes. He may seem unable even to sit on a chair in an ordinary way. His speech may be so interspersed with slang and adolescent jargon as to be almost unintelligible to his parents. He may appear lazy and listless, or show spurts of activity. In short, his behaviour is unpredictable, full of contradictions, a series of puzzles.

It is this puzzling adolescent who needs understanding. Otherwise, his parents may fail him when he needs them most. It is so easy to slip into the habit of nagging at the adolescent, to act as though his expressions of insecurity were deliberate attempts to annoy his parents. This is a time in the life of the child when his parents should overlook the relatively unimportant things, even if they are irritating. The most frequent complaint of the adolescent is that his parents treat him like a child. Often he means by this that they check up on his table manners, his way of dressing, his language and many other similar things. However, even though he behaves in a childish way at times, he still wants to be treated as an adult.

Actually some of the adolescent's puzzling behaviour stems from the fact that he is trying to be both dependent and independent. He is reluctant to lose the feeling of security he gets from having his parents make decisions for him, but at the same time he wants the feeling of independence that comes from reduced supervision. He is trying to go in two directions at the same time. Nevertheless, parents should realize that the more the adolescent is treated like an adult, the more he will try to act like one.

Now adolescence is not just an incident in growing up. Rather it is a fairly long period in the life of the boy or girl, lasting for at least five or six years. The expressions of insecurity mentioned above will not necessarily last over the whole period, but they are almost certain to appear at some time. We, as parents, should look for indications of increasing maturity in control and responsibility; and the adolescent needs to know that we are aware of and satisfied with these.

During adolescence, several motives come to the fore: the drive for independence, the desire for acceptance by contemporaries, the desire to feel that progress is being made, the want to feel self-important, the desire to be creative or to excel in something. Our society, however, allows very little opportunity for the satisfaction of these motives. Usually an enthusiastic reformer, the adolescent has no chance to reform the world with which he is dissatisfied. When he would like to go on some exciting crusade, he is told to buckle down to his homework. Consequently, we often find the adolescent restless and impatient with his school and his teachers, frequently annoyed at his parents, and generally out of sorts with the world. Yes, the adolescent does need sympathetic understanding!

Today, perhaps more than in any previous period in our history, parents are unsure. They have been confused by the rapid changes in the meaning of parental authority and methods of bringing up children. This unsureness about the effectiveness of their methods has been reflected in less faith in their adolescents. Because they have felt insecure as parents, they have frequently lacked faith in their grownup children, and have tried to continue directing their behaviour longer than is desirable. The adolescent has been vaguely aware of this lack of trust, and it has added to his own insecurity and uncertainty. Adolescents need sympathetic understanding and trust from parents and teachers. It is true at all ages, but even more so during adolescence, that to expect the best helps to produce the best.

A central principle of child training can be stated as the gradual progressive shift of control from without to within the child. Every month should bring increased areas of responsibility and self-discipline. Adolescence is the final stage in this process, so that for the older adolescent there will be very few areas of decision and activity that are not his own responsibility. External control will have given way to advice and guidance. To lay down the law to the adolescent, to demand that he follow the parental dictates is to invite open rebellion, smoldering resentment, or deceit.

A too authoritative approach has the even more serious result of usually shutting off effective communication and thus blocking contact with the adolescent. In talking to parents of adolescents, I have frequently been told, "But I can't talk to my son or daughter. They won't listen to me." And some adolescents have said the same about their parents: "I just can't talk to them. They won't listen to me." This is unfortunate because discussion provides the most effective method of helping the adolescent. Parents who have kept the channels of communication open testify to the reasonableness of their teen-age children in talking over problems. It is rather easy for parents to fall into the habit of first saying "No" to everything the young people ask or suggest, and then becoming involved in an argument which they frequently lose. It is much more desirable and effective to meet each such situation with, "Well, I don't know – let's talk it over." It is almost always possible to find an acceptable compromise, and at the same time to give the adolescent the feeling that his parents are not against him but are reasonable and open-minded, especially if the discussion is carried on not as a kind of battle, but as a real attempt to find a solution that is best for all concerned.

One of the most puzzling things for the parent to understand is the seeming disregard of his wishes and commands. The parent often fails to realize that the adolescent wants to follow these wishes and suggestions, but is simply unable to do so because he has other standards which to him are even more important than his parents' wishes. For example, here is a young lady of sixteen, whose parents think she should be home from a party by eleven o'clock; but at eleven her hostess is just starting to serve the lunch. Can she leave and drag her escort with her? What will the group think of her if she does? Will she ever get another invitation? She knows her parents will be annoyed and perhaps forbid her going out again for awhile. She is in a difficult spot. She decides that it is easier to stay and take a chance on what will happen later. Unfortunately, however, her parents do not even listen to her and there are hard words, resentment, and misunderstanding.

Or again, here is a young man of fifteen, whose mother has definite ideas about what he should wear, ideas that are rather different from those of the crowd. The adolescent wants to follow his mother's wishes, but he cannot do so because the other standards are more important to him. A battle results. If the boy wins, he may have to live with a mother who "puts on a martyr act" and implies that she is hurt and disappointed in a son who is "ungrateful enough to go against my wishes – after all I have done for him, too!"

These may seem to be relatively unimportant incidents, and yet it is this kind of misunderstanding that influences parent-adolescent relationships. It is just as easy and much more effective for the parent to try to talk over with the adolescent these everyday situations, try to see his point of view, and thus arrive at solutions which are acceptable to both.

Parents and teachers who fail to take the time to try to understand adolescents are puzzled by them, but bewilderment gives place to sympathetic understanding when the adult can see things through the eyes of the teen-ager. This is what the adolescent needs most of all. He does not need or want a lot of help and advice, but he does need moral support. He needs to feel that his parents and teachers are on his side, that they have faith in him, that they are pulling for him. He needs a feeling of security in his own home, a feeling that there he is understood and accepted and liked. He needs to feel that he is wanted at school, that his thoughts and aspirations are respected, and that the school is there to help him achieve some of the things he hopes for in life.

Adolescents need be neither puzzles nor problems, but they do require understanding. Any real attempt to understand their motives and problems, their struggles and fumbles will pay large dividends.

Achieving maturity[4]

Adolescence is the last stage on the way to maturity. But full maturity is not just a matter of age, nor does it come as a matter of course; it must be won. This period in the struggle for maturity is one of the most puzzling and difficult for parents to understand and deal with, and it requires the most careful and intelligent handling.

What is maturity? There are a number of answers to this question. The laws of our land state that a person has achieved a maturity which makes him capable of taking part in the affairs of his country when he is twenty-one, for then he may vote. But age is a doubtful criterion of maturity. Children "come of age" for some purposes when they are eighteen, for example, to marry and start a new family. At sixteen the child is relieved of curfew laws and compulsory school attendance and is old enough to drive a car. A boy or girl may enlist in the armed forces at eighteen. There are, of course, some peculiar features in this use of chronological age as the standard. A boy may be old enough to fight and die for his country but not old enough to vote, and a boy and girl who

4 K. S. Bernhardt, "Achieving maturity," *Parent Educ. Bull.*, 1944, no. 27, 2 – 6.

are old enough to marry and have a family may not be old enough to help decide the affairs of the nation. So in our discussion of maturity we shall discard the use of age as a criterion.

In place of age we shall use a more indefinite standard. We shall say that a person is mature when he is fully developed physically, intellectually, emotionally, and socially. Such an individual is capable of making his own decisions and running his own life satisfactorily. He can adjust happily and efficiently in a world with other people: he has learned how to get along with others. He is in control of his emotional life: he rules his emotions instead of being ruled by them. He has discarded temper tantrums and tears as methods of social control. His controls are internal rather than external. He has learned how to control his environment instead of letting his environment control him. He has purposes and ideals: he knows what he wants and gives a meaning to the business of living.

Such maturity does not just happen, it is achieved. And not everyone achieves it. It is the product of long training and much practice. It is the goal of all education from infancy on. The training in self-help and making choices, in requirements and consequences, of the pre-school period, and the development of skills and understanding in the school-age period are or should be directed towards this important end. If these early years are effectively used, the final stages in the process should not be difficult, but because we so often fail in this foundation training the years of later adolescence are often difficult for youth, parents, and teachers.

Parents, teachers, and other adults are becoming more and more aware of the importance of intelligent guidance for the older adolescent. But such guidance is only possible when there is an understanding of the problems, difficulties, and specific needs of these young people. Most of us are aware of the lack of rapport between youth and adults, of the noisy boisterousness and the rebellion against authority that so frequently characterize youth, but very few of us understand what motivates such behaviour. Because of this lack of understanding it is customary to blame youth for its thoughtlessness. This impatience with the adolescent merely serves to aggravate the situation and to make it more urgent for the adolescent to fight for his place in the sun.

Understanding youth means understanding and taking into account the fundamental wants that are the universal possession of young men and women. These wants can be stated briefly. (1) They want to be accepted – to feel that they belong, to feel that they are secure in the affections of parents and teachers as well as of contemporaries. They want and need this emotional anchor. (2) They want approval. This follows from (1), but should be mentioned separately. They want to be appreciated as individuals – to feel that they have something to contribute that is important to and appreciated by others. (3) Related to this is their want for the feeling of achievement, progress, and accomplishment. There is nothing quite so satisfying at any age as the excitement of achievement and during later adolescence it must be experienced or there is dissatisfaction, unrest, and often blind groping that is productive of conflict. (4) They want to be and feel important. This want often has rather far-reaching results and sometimes rather unfortunate expressions. (5) The older adolescents want to be independent. They want to be thought of and treated as grown-ups, not as children.

Now, how can these wants be taken into account? Let us look at them one at a time. Adolescents need to be emotionally secure in their homes. They need to feel that they are safe in the affections of their parents. This doesn't mean that they should be treated as children, or that affection must be on display, but it does mean that the boy or girl should be made to feel that there is an abiding permanent affection that is not touched by anything he may do.

Feelings of inferiority are much too frequent in adolescents. In fact, it might be said that feelings of inferiority are the common lot of all young men and women. This is not obvious to the casual observer, because a youth often tries to cover his feelings of inferiority with a crust of boisterous, noisy bluster. But get beneath this surface and you will find that he feels unsure of himself. We can help these young people by the frequent use of approval and appreciation of their efforts. Another manifestation of this feeling of inferiority is that the young man or young woman must be "in the swim". He may suffer agonies if he can't wear the same kind of clothes, use the same kind of language, do the same kind of things, and keep the same late hours as the other members of his "gang." He must have that feeling of belonging and acceptance that comes from conformity and conformity to the adolescent means doing what the gang does, wearing what the gang wears, and even using the latest slang.

There is nothing quite so effective in making life worth living as a feeling of achievement. Often the older adolescent has difficulty in attaining this feeling of accomplishment. However, we are beginning to learn how to manage education so that these young men and women can feel that they are making progress, that they are achieving some things that are worthwhile. When all the tasks are chosen by someone else, and when it is only necessary to do what someone else plans for you, this feeling of achievement is hard to gain. There is more room in school and home for the self-chosen task so that boys and girls may experience the excitement that comes from achieving something that they want to achieve.

There's nothing quite so conducive to feelings of unrest and dissatisfaction as being left out of important happenings. Many a sixteen and seventeen year old has felt that way lately. There is much that they can do, and much that can be done to make them feel that they are important. Instead of telling these boys and girls "You're not old enough yet" or "Wait a few years," we could suggest ways in which they could be made to feel important.

Adolescents want to grow up. They want the independence that they think should go with their size. The most bothersome thing to young people is being treated like children – being told what to do, when to do it, and how to do it. Parents are often proud of their grown-up children, doing everything possible to further their physical maturity, but at the same time doing nothing or very little to promote their emotional maturity. In many cases parents try to hinder the attempt to be independent. When we see a sixteen-year old boy who is well behaved, docile, and obedient, letting his parents make all his decisions for him, we feel like telling him "For goodness sake, don't let these parents of yours run your whole life – break away and decide some things for yourself."

Parents and teachers need to gradually apportion more responsibility to the adolescent. Youth should not have to fight for his independence, but if he doesn't get it any other way he should fight. The days of telling are over or should be. These young people now need counsellors and friends, not dictators.

Conflict between the teen-age boy or girl and the parents is almost inevitable if the parents "lay down the law" about hours, friends, and related problems. These are matters for guidance rather than for law. Frequently we find that serious conflict occurs between parents and their teen-age children over relatively unimportant issues. These clashes can often be avoided if such issues are overlooked and more important things are discussed. Most adolescents react well to reasonable guidance and leadership. Difficulties arise because the adult concerned tries to boss. Many an adolescent can be led who won't be driven.

Companionship poses a very common problem. Many a parent has thought that some boy is not suitable to associate with their daughter, or that their son is being led astray by his companions. Usually they forbid such companionship – with the usual results. Resentment and misunderstanding arise and the forbidden friends become even more romantic and desirable. A more effective method is that of encouraging the boy or girl to bring their friends home. Adolescents must feel free to choose their own friends and shouldn't be driven to hiding their associations from their parents.

The community as a whole must accept the responsibility for the provision of more wholesome recreational opportunities for youth. Every community must make sure that there are adequate facilities for healthy recreation for boys and girls. The home, the school, the church and the community as a whole can help youth to achieve maturity by providing an abundance of chances for young men and young women to find satisfying leisure time activities.

A number of questions might be asked, the answers to which would give some indication of how well the young man or woman will be able to adjust to life.

1   Has he an adventurous, exploratory spirit? Does he welcome new experiences, new ideas, and new tasks?

2   Does he have a desire to be strong and healthy? Does he take pride in a strong, clean, healthy body?

3   Does he like to be with people? Is he interested in people? Can he talk and listen?

4   Has he some hobbies that he is enthusiastic about and which do not depend too much on circumstances and materials? Can he amuse himself?

5   Does he make his own decisions? Has he initiative? Can he accept the responsibility for planning and carrying through projects?

6   Does he know and care about the basic principles of democratic living?

7   Has he drive, ambition and ideals? Has he formulated a philosophy of life? Does he know what he wants from living?

The answers to these questions might be taken as something of a criterion of how effective the home has been and is being in helping the young man or woman to achieve maturity.

There are a number of suggestions which might be offered to youth.

If followed, they would aid greatly in this difficult process of growing into maturity. I offer these suggestions here so that parents, teachers, and others may consider them in the light of their contacts with teen-age boys and girls.

1   Youth must get out of the clutches of possessive parents. This can be achieved by helping the parents to develop other interests so that their lives are not completely wrapped up in their children. It can be helped also by the adolescents leaving home for school, camp, work, or merely on a visit.

2   Earning money and managing an income also aids maturity.

3   The teen-age boy or girl can be helped by association with the opposite sex in co-educational activities and in "dating." The mature person is "at home" with both sexes.

4   Taking part in organized social activities is helpful, especially if the individual assumes some responsibility for planning the activities.

5   The adolescent needs to practice the art of losing gracefully and recognizing superiority, in other words, the skill of fellowship.

6   The attainment of maturity is aided by the necessity of making decisions for oneself.

7   Tolerance for differences in customs, attitudes, and ideas is another sign of developing maturity.

8   The acquisition of the skills valued by the group, such as dancing and skiing, is important.

9   Willingness to postpone satisfactions and to work for future goals helps the individual to grow up.

10 The development of a philosophy of life which is not just a copy of someone else's beliefs but the product of his own thinking and experience indicates that the adolescent is growing up.

To sum up, the mature individual is grown up physically, mentally, socially, and emotionally. He is emancipated from his parents. He has achieved a satisfactory adjustment to the opposite sex. He has learned to appreciate the attitudes and behaviour of others. He is capable of delaying his responses. He has learned to control his emotions. He manages his environment instead of being a slave to it. He has a philosophy of life. The business of home, school, and community is to provide opportunities for youth to achieve this kind of maturity.

Chapter 6

Discipline

OF THE MANY TOPICS covered over the years in the articles by Karl Bernhardt the three which received the most parental interest were discipline, character development, and sex education, the subjects of this and the next three chapters. Perhaps the most discussed topic in Karl Bernhardt's articles is that of discipline. A complete exposition of his approach to and philosophy of discipline can be found in his 1964 book *Discipline and Child Care*.

In this chapter parts of a number of articles written throughout the years on this important subject have been assembled. The last section is from an article by David Bernhardt which attempts to apply the philosophy to the field of education.

Throughout these articles the dominant theme is that of developing within the child some form of intelligent self-discipline. This is done best by formulating a disciplinary scheme in which the consequences flow out of the situations. The key words are consistency, immediacy, invariability, and logical relationship with the behaviour of the child.

In the following chapter, "Discipline Problems," a number of the day-to-day problems which the parent must face when children misbehave are explored in the light of the philosophy of discipline outlined here.

Freedom and discipline[1]

Freedom and discipline are words which evoke highly emotional responses. They are also words with many meanings. On the surface they seem to be antithetical but I suggest that they stand for two essential ingredients of a training which leads to a maturity of self-discipline which is essentially self-fulfilment.

It is obvious that human freedom must be interpreted within a framework of social living and that membership in any society imposes both demands and restrictions which make doing "whatever one pleases" an impossibility. Yet the freedom of individual choice and decision is one of our treasured privileges. This, then, is one of the challenges to man's intelligence and ingenuity – to build a society and a way of life

1 K. S. Bernhardt, "Freedom and discipline as a means toward self-discipline," *Bull. Inst. Child Stud.*, 1960, 22(3), 2–4.

on the seeming contradiction of freedom and discipline. Perhaps this is the society we like to call democratic.

Just as freedom and self-discipline are the characteristics of a democratic way of life, so freedom and discipline are the training devices to be used in preparing youth for participation in a democratic society: freedom to grow, learn, choose, and experience but in such a way that the same freedom for others is not hindered or restricted. Freedom and discipline are like Siamese twins who flourish when linked together but die when separated. Freedom without discipline is anarchy, and discipline without freedom is basically unjust.

In the past several decades some people have discovered that love is not enough, that tender loving care is just the beginning and not the be-all of bringing up children, and that frustration does not always result in neuroses.

Of course children need love, but children also need discipline. Child rearing has focused more and more on the end result, on growing up, on maturity. Such a focus can be beneficial but it can also lead to some misplaced emphases. With some few (and almost pathological) exceptions, adults (parents and teachers) have been impatient for children to grow up. We do not like childhood with its immaturity, childish behaviour, ignorance and ineptitude. We want children to be good little miniature adults; we tend to treat them that way and are disappointed when they still act their age.

The central core of child rearing is, of course, discipline. Around this concept some of the sharpest controversies have swirled. This is not surprising since the views we hold on discipline determine practically every detail of what we do and how we do it in the process of bringing up children.

Perhaps it is because discipline is so central and so fundamental that sharp differences of opinion have occurred. These differences often lead to confusion and wide swings of the pendulum in practice. There can be no doubt that the last three or four decades have witnessed, in North America particularly, rather startling changes in emphasis in child rearing – swings from one extreme to another with little evidence of a stabilizing middle-of-the-road position. It may be that there is no real middle ground between what is essentially a punitive approach and one that is realistically educational.

We have lived so long with the punitive approach that it is difficult for us to think in other terms. Perhaps this is because it is so difficult to develop a deep abiding faith in mankind. Perhaps we still believe that man is by nature bad, sinful, and depraved and feel that the only avenue to understanding is essentially biological, sensory, and pleasure-pain. The punitive approach implies this. It is interesting that some of the recent rat research on learning seems to be saying the same thing. However, surely we need to keep reminding ourselves that our children are something other than rats. It is time we advanced beyond the approach Watson took, more than thirty years ago, when he implied a kind of passive mechanism which could be conditioned to act in the way desired.

Freud's approach has also led to confusion. It set hundreds of clinicians searching in the dark for unconscious motives that mysteriously produced behaviour seemingly contrary to the desires of the behaver.

Today, however, there is almost unanimity on one point and that is on our goal in bringing up children. We are trying to produce self-disciplined, mature, socialized adults – people who can run their own lives satisfactorily and who do not require a whole complicated set of external controls. That we have failed to do this is evident on all sides. A simple test of our failure: how many people today drive their cars the same way when they know there is no policeman in sight as when they think a policeman is near?

If our goal is to produce self-disciplined adults, then our problem is to discover how to do it. Perhaps examination of what self-discipline means will give us a clue. Among other things it means self-control and self-direction, responsibility, dependability, with no need for supervision, check-up, or external control. In other words, the control is from within – not the control of fear of being caught and punished but rather the control of understanding and acceptance of sensible, necessary standards, rules and laws.

If we want intelligent conformity rather than conformity through fear or conformity as an end in itself, then we must somehow cultivate the understanding which is its foundation. This will take time, but time is always provided for this job of bringing up children. We usually have from fifteen to twenty years to complete the job.

Picture a helpless, ignorant, immature infant who we hope will become a self-disciplined mature adult! What happens to him in those years will tell the story. This is our belief: that the infant will become the kind of person he does because of the training he receives, even though we know vaguely that heredity too will have something to do with it.

Permissiveness?[2]

Before we parents have had time to recover from one slogan or catch-word, we are confronted with another. There has been a series of them: free-expression, self-realization, self-demand, and now, permissiveness. To be a permissive parent is the current fashion. The originators of the plan of permissiveness probably never intended that a whole programme of child training should be based on it. The idea came first from the clinic. It was found that many children with serious problems responded very well in an atmosphere in which they were free to do as they wished, to express their anxieties and hostilities in overt form, and to be ac-cepted whatever they did. Permissive sessions of play therapy were used with some children; a permissive therapeutic institution became the home of others when everything else had failed (Bettelheim 1955). These children had grown up in unfavourable environments, which had been either over-regimented or completely disorganized. A high degree of permissiveness was used as treatment (although some limits or boundaries of action were always set), and in many cases it worked with almost miraculous effect.

Many lay people have heard about permissiveness, but they have erred in attempting to use a form of psychological therapy as a general and complete plan of guidance for their well children. It is as if, having heard that high dosages of vitamin B were good for certain physical illnesses, we decided to give it to our perfectly healthy children.

The idea of permissiveness, however, has a real place in our plan for bringing up children. Let us therefore examine some of the ways in which we have sometimes misused it, and also consider in what ways it can be of real value.

Being permissive can mean a number of things. It can mean letting the child develop at his own rate without undue pressures or attempts to hurry him. It can mean discarding blame and recrimination, and never correcting or punishing the child for his behaviour. It has also been taken to mean that one should let the child do as he likes, without restraint and direction. In this last sense, a permissive parent is one who lets nature take its course, denying the child the steadying hand of direction and supervision.

2 K. S. Bernhardt, "How permissive are you?" *Bull. Inst. Child Stud.*, 1956, 18(2), 1–6.

The complete use of such ideas as free-expression, self-demand, and permissiveness are, in effect, a denial of the need or desirability of training. They suggest that it is important to let the child's personality unfold by itself. This, in turn, seems to rest on a kind of blind faith in nature, heredity, maturation, or on some process that will take care of things if we do not interfere. However, a knowledge of development will not allow us to maintain such faith. The individual is the product of a number of influences, among which are, of course, constitutional or hereditary factors. But these are by no means the whole story. The kinds of experience which the child has also play a large part in his development. The child who is allowed to do whatever he likes becomes the adult with little sense of responsibility, one who may fail to consider the rights and feelings of others. I watched a brash young ten-year-old push his way into a line ahead of hundreds of others, and when someone pointed out to him that he should take his place at the end of the line as the rest had done, he merely shrugged his shoulders and said he didn't have to, that he would do as he liked. He is possibly the product of a home in which the parents had thought they were being permissive whereas actually they were letting the child do as he wanted, without restraint or direction.

To be a happy, efficient member of society implies a level of self-discipline that is seen in living by the rules, taking other people into account, and curbing personal desires in favour of group goals. This can only happen through a planned discipline that provides opportunities to both understand and abide by the sensible rules of social life. The main point is that the child, because he is a child, cannot always know what is best for himself or the group to which he belongs. True, his parents and teachers do not always know either, but they have a better chance of knowing than the child. Obviously, if we want to keep him safe and sound and have him learn how to live with other people, the child cannot be allowed always to do as he pleases.

The other side of the picture is equally important. The child whose desires are frequently thwarted, whose activity is so hemmed in with rules and prohibitions that he can have no feeling of freedom or self-direction, shows the results of this in his resentments, his rebellion, and his aggression.

What does all this mean for the parent who wants to "do the best" for the child? It means the use of both permissiveness and discipline, stepping in and also keeping hands off. In other words, it is not as simple as choosing between discipline and permissiveness. It is not a question of one or the other, but of both. The real problem is to know how to arrive at the right mixture, to know when to be permissive and when to direct or prohibit. To further complicate the picture, the proportions of permissiveness and discipline have to change as the child learns and progresses towards maturity.

How can we decide when to be permissive and when to interfere and direct, require, or prohibit? We can get an answer to this by considering the functions and meaning of parenthood, the nature of the child, and the goals we are working for. Parents are faced with the challenging job of protecting the child until he can look after himself, seeing that he has opportunities to learn how to manage his own affairs, guiding him from childish selfishness towards becoming a socialized person, and seeing that he keeps moving gradually towards self-disciplined maturity. Children do not become adults automatically. They do so when they have had sufficient practice in directing their own behaviour, and when the consequences of what they do are such that the practice results in the right kind of learning. Here is a simple example.

A little child wants an ice cream cone. His mother says "No, not now." The child kicks and screams, and finally the mother gets him the cone to keep him quiet. What has the child learned? He has learned that to kick and scream is one way of getting what he wants. He learns to connect his own behaviour with its results. This is how he learns most things. He remembers what leads to success and what leads to failure. If we want the child to learn how to live in a complex world with other people, there are some situations in which we cannot be permissive. The small child who throws his food on the floor can learn that when he does this he goes hungry until the next meal; but he can learn that there are right and wrong ways and places to use them. So, obviously, permissiveness is not a universal rule. Some behaviour is not permissible.

Permissiveness is sometimes a reaction from a strict, cold, autocratic, command-obey kind of discipline. Discarding one scheme, however, does not necessarily mean that we have to go to the opposite extreme; in fact, extremes are usually undesirable in this area. It is not necessary to discard all control just because some people have made control too stringent. Some control is absolutely necessary with young children. The important question is how this control is to be exercised and in what situations.

Children like to know where they stand, to know what is allowed and what is out of bounds. To be completely permissive throws too heavy a burden on young shoulders. A minimum set of planned, reasonable requirements which the child must accept is not only a good idea but a necessity, if the child is to develop in a healthy way. These requirements should be clearly understood by the child and enforced in a consistent manner. The main principle of their administration is the use of reasonable arbitrary consequences for non-conformity, that is when the child fails to live up to a known requirement he suffers some logical consequence or result. For example, when he cannot abide by the rules of the social group, he cannot be a member of that group until he is ready to accept the rules. In this way, he learns that each situation makes demands on him, and that there is an appropriate way of behaving in it. Permissiveness may give him the impression that his behaviour is subject to the whims of mother, father, or teacher, who generously permit him to do certain things. What we want him to learn is that he himself chooses to behave in certain ways, and that if his choices are undesirable he will suffer the consequences of his unwise choices.

Permissiveness has a very definite place in those areas that do not involve requirements. Here the child can feel that the adult not only permits but welcomes his free choice of activities. A sense of freedom and self-direction is valuable, and should be encouraged whenever possible. Of course, even in such free activity situations there have to be limits and boundaries and even rules, but these rules and limits can be made to contribute to, rather than hinder, the feeling of freedom.

One of the reasons why permissiveness does not appeal to me as a guiding concept is that it seems to cast the parent in such a passive role. It seems to say that the adult, out of the goodness of his heart, allows the child to do things. The parent becomes a kind of benevolent onlooker, but the parent's role, as I see it, is far from passive. It is very definitely an active one in which he provides, directs, supervises, and, where necessary, arranges arbitrary consequences to aid the child's learning. Permissiveness seems to leave out this active interest and participation which is so vital a part of being a parent. However, it does imply that instead of telling the child everything he should or must do, the parent plans and arranges situations so that the child can make some of his own choices. It is not, then, a matter of being either permissive or autocratic, but rather of knowing when it is wise to be permissive and when it is necessary to enforce rules and requirements.

Another aspect of the permissive idea is the relationship between adult and child: the parent-child or teacher-child relationship. Our increasing knowledge of child development points to the value of a warm, trusting, sympathetic relationship. At one time, adults thought that it was necessary to be cold and distant in order to maintain control. The old picture of a good disciplinarian was that of a fearsome, unbending, unfriendly, remote figure who dispensed painful punishment for any sign of disobedience. We know now that to strike terror into the heart of a child in order to maintain control is a very dangerous technique for any parent or teacher. However, we know too that it is not necessary to forego all regulation in dispensing with the use of fear and intimidation. A parent or teacher can be warm and friendly and still be consistent and just in enforcing sensible, necessary requirements. Warmth and affection do not necessarily mean indulging the child's every whim. This is the danger in the permissive concept. It has meant to some parents that they must not make demands on the child, that they must be indulgent even when it is not in the best interests of the child.

Children thrive in an atmosphere in which they feel wanted and liked. It is not possible to love a child too much, but it is rather easy to misuse love, or to let love stand in the way of helping the child become a responsible, self-disciplined individual. It is both possible and necessary to blend love, justice, and consistency. It is a misuse of love to try to control the child by such statements or implications as "Mother can only love you when you are good." Love need not stand in the way of seeing that the child experiences the logical results of his own nonconformity. Rules, requirements, and prohibitions that are reasonable and necessary and that are consistently enforced need not interfere with this warm, friendly, affectionate relationship. Indeed the reverse is true, for the child's trust in the parent, which is a part of this relationship, develops best on the foundation of a reasonable, consistent plan of discipline.

Coming back to our original question, "How permissive are you?" We are not now thinking in narrow terms of merely letting the child do what he likes; we are thinking of helping the child grow and learn. We are thinking of being on good terms with the child, understanding him, having faith in him, and giving him a chance to have faith in us. Children need to feel that we are with them and for them, that we are their friends as well as their parents and teachers. At the same time they must have the direction and regulation that give them a feeling of knowing where they stand, what they can do, and what is out of bounds. This is the most challenging and the most important part of parenthood: to be able to blend reasonable control with sensible permissiveness.

Rewards and punishment?[3]

There has been more discussion and confusion about the use of rewards and punishments than about any other single phase of child training. They have the approval of age, tradition, and long use. However, we cannot accept any technique merely because of its age; we must find some better criterion for its evaluation. In the search for such a standard of evaluation there is one preliminary question that must be answered – what results are we looking for? If it is immediate results we desire, then it must be said that rewards and punishments are fairly effective in most cases, and, furthermore, they are rather simple to use. There is no doubt that one of the simplest ways of getting the child to do something is to offer a large enough and attractive enough reward. There is no doubt either that in most cases severe punishment will prevent the child from repeating an undesirable activity.

I am assuming, however, that immediate results are not the only consideration. As parents and teachers we are even more interested in the long-term results on the character and personality of the child. Immediate results are, of course, important but not as important as the effects of the present situation on the personality of the developing child. I am assuming, also, that as parents and teachers we have a definite goal, and that the goal can be expressed in some such terms as the following. The purpose of child training and education is to produce well-adjusted, emotionally and socially mature adults, who are capable of running their own lives satisfactorily, making their own decisions, and abiding by the consequences of these decisions and activities. It is in the light of such a goal that we can evaluate techniques such as rewards and punishments. We will consider anything that contributes to the attainment of this goal a good technique and anything that hinders the attainment of this goal a poor technique to be discarded in favour of a better one.

Now we are ready to look in detail at the use of rewards and punishments. We shall consider rewards first. What is a reward and what is the main reason for using it? A reward is some tangible expression of approval of the individual's behaviour. It is used in order to produce a repetition of a desirable form of activity. In this form it is in the nature of a bribe or inducement to direct activity. Implicit in the use of reward

3 K. S. Bernhardt, "The use of rewards and punishments in child training," *Parent Educ. Bull.*, 1944, no. 29, 3–6.

is the idea that if an individual can be induced to perform a specific activity a number of times a habit will be formed.

An expression of approval of desirable activity may aid the individual to learn what is socially acceptable and what is not, and in that sense there is some justification for the reward as an emphatic expression of social approval. However, rewards are not the only method by which the child can learn what is acceptable to the society in which he lives. Whether what he does is accepted or not can be learned better in terms of the natural consequences of his own behaviour. There is the ever-present danger that a reward will become a bribe, and a bribe tells the child that the activity is unpleasant or difficult and that we cannot justly expect him to do it without some addition, some inducement. In other words, we tell him that the activity is not worthwhile in itself and must be made so by the offer of some artificial incentive. Being good is not worthwhile in itself, so we will make it worthwhile by adding a reward of ten cents a week for good behaviour. Eating vegetables is too unpleasant so we will make it more pleasant by adding an inducement such as an ice cream cone. Regular attendance at Sunday School is not worthwhile in itself, so we will add to it a reward of a book or some other prize. Doing well in school carries no feeling of accomplishment, so we will add a medal or scholarship. Rewards, then, tend to obscure the issue. They make it difficult for the child to learn that there are some things that are worth doing for themselves, and that there are other activities which must be performed whether we like them or not because they are a necessary part of the business of living.

The idea that repeated performance of an activity is habit-forming is based on a wrong conception of learning. We learn what we practise, not what we do. Take, for example, a child who is offered a reward for tidiness. He keeps his belongings tidy in order to win the reward. He is being tidy but he is practising not tidiness but winning rewards, and what he learns is not necessarily to be tidy but to work for rewards. In fact, it is quite possible that he is learning that he can gain rewards by being untidy and that his distracted parent will in desperation offer an attractive bribe. It is the experience of many parents and teachers that rewards once begun must be continued, for their removal is the signal for the return to old ways.

The use of rewards inevitably produces in the child the "reward habit." The child learns to expect a reward and to work only when one is offered. Start a child with the idea that his school work is evaluated with gold stars, prizes, and other rewards and soon you will have a child who sees no value in any work which does not bring some artificial result. The author's experience with children has taught him that children soon learn to ask "What's there in it for me, what do I get?" The child should be helped to discover as soon as possible that life consists of two kinds of activities – those things that he must do whether he likes doing them or not (the necessary things of living) and those things he does only because he likes doing them. To reward the child for the performance of the requirements of living is to obscure the fact that they are requirements, and to reward a child for doing the things that he likes to do is not only superfluous but distracting.

In terms of our goal – producing mature adults – rewards hinder rather than help. Child training and education would be much more effective if all rewards were abolished. The child does not need to lose out because of this. There is no reason why, for instance, he can't be provided with all the books, ice cream, and play materials that he requires without "earning" them as rewards. One final thought about rewards. When a reward is offered to a group, usually only one member of the group can win it and the others, even though some of them may have worked just as hard as the winner, are left out in the cold.

Punishments present some of the same problems as rewards. They are artificial incentives designed to keep the child from repeating undesirable activity. Often they tend to obscure the real issues involved. There are three possible reasons for the use of punishments: (1) as revenge, (2) as a deterrent, and (3) as a method of reform. No one likes the sound of the word "revenge" and certainly we can discard this as a reason for the use of punishment. Punishment as a method of deterring people from wrongdoing is sometimes effective, sometimes rather ineffective. Whether it works or not in this way is less important than what it does to the individual in terms of character and personality. The individual who is kept from doing wrong by fear and who abides by the rules and regulations of society only because he is afraid of the punishment he might receive if he is caught is not a very effective member of that society. Much better that he should learn to understand and appreciate the meaning and value of the laws and accept them as necessary regulations, thus conforming not because of fear but because of desire. Finally, punishment as a method of reform has been much overrated. Very few individuals are reformed because they have been punished. We are gradually moving in our society to the point where the person who breaks the laws of society is studied and a programme of treatment is used instead of a programme of punishment. This trend should also apply in the field of child training and education.

Punishment is usually a personal and emotional technique. That is, the child is punished by someone and that someone is often angry and the whole situation is so charged with emotion that the child fails to learn what is desired from him. Punishment is generally resented by the person who receives it. This resentment is focused on the person handing out the punishment and thus the relationship between the child and the parent or teacher is weakened. Punishment always implies blame and disapproval: the child has made a mistake or he has failed to live up to some requirement. By punishing this child we imply that we think he should be able to do better, but the real reason for his mistake is often merely his immaturity. He still has much to learn.

How can we get along without using punishments? This question gives the impression that punishments are the only means we have for directing children. This is not the case. Also, many people think that without punishments children must be allowed to do what they like. Again this is not true. We can make use of what I like to call consequences, even though it is a rather awkward term. By consequences we mean that the child should suffer the impersonal, logical results of his own lack of conformity. Often the consequence appears to be the same as a punishment, but the difference lies mainly in the attitude of the adult. The attitude of the adult in using punishment is one of blaming the child, thinking of him as bad and deserving of pain. The child is in disgrace. On the other hand, the consequence follows his own behaviour as a matter of course. He has brought it on himself and it is not in any way dependent on the whim or feeling of the adult. Sometimes the adult has to be the agency which administers or brings about the consequence, but even when this is necessary it can be administered in an impersonal manner so that the child can feel that it is a result of his own behaviour. It is very important to keep in mind that the child needs to learn that every situation makes demands on him in some way, and that if he fails to live up to these demands there are inevitable consequences that accrue to him. Parents and teachers then cease to be stern dictators who will become angry and punish the offender if their will is not accepted, and become friendly guides and mentors who help the child to learn to live up to the necessary rules and requirements of society.

In those homes and schools where rewards and punishments have been discarded and more intelligent techniques employed the children do not run wild and they do learn and develop. Without rewards the children are usually more interested in learning itself. Consequently we do not hesitate to advocate a trial of techniques other than rewards and punishments.

A reasonable scheme of discipline[4]

To most people discipline has a forbidding sound because to them it means correction and punishment. The Oxford Dictionary gives seven different meanings of the word, the first being teaching, and the seventh, correction. It is the first or original meaning of the word that is being used in this chapter. Discipline is a plan of training, the arranging of conditions for learning. When we think of discipline as correction and punishment, it become a mixture of pain, unpleasantness, emotional upsets, fear and inhibitions, but, it is thought, a necessary part of child rearing and education. This is not positive, reasonable discipline, but a distortion of it. It is a largely negative concept and usually ineffectual in the long run.

Discipline can be positive, helpful, and reasonable, when we think of it as a plan of training rather than merely a way of dealing with undesirable behaviour. The need for discipline arises from the simple fact that some of the wants and impulses of the individual may run counter to his safety and welfare as well as to the demands of the society in which he lives. The individual has to learn to shape his behaviour so as to balance his own wants and the limitations and restrictions demanded by the society in which he lives as well as the dangers and realities of his environment. In other words, unhampered freedom is unrealistic. Actually freedom is only possible in a context of responsibility.

Both discipline and child rearing in general have varied with the changing views and attitudes of the culture. The more complex society is, the more difficult and confusing child rearing becomes. The guiding principles of a scheme of discipline reflect the dominant views, attitudes, and social philosophy of the times. Thus, today's methods reflect the insecurity, confusion, and uncertainty of society. This is indicated by the question most frequently asked by parents, "What is the right thing to do when ... ?"

Parents want simple, easy, concrete rules to follow. When the values, goals, and principles are not clear, then people look for some simple formula. But the rules can be misleading rather than helpful if the goals and principles are confused, and when every situation is different and

4 K. S. Bernhardt, "A positive, non-punitive scheme of discipline," *Bull. Inst. Child Stud.*, 1962, 24(3), 1–9.

when the children show great individual differences, rules are not adequate. Adults must have not a simple formula but flexible principles and clear goals.

What should I do with my daughter who is irresponsible, doesn't help around the house, and neglects her school work? No rule can answer this question. The parent faced with this "problem" could find some of the answers by developing a sympathetic understanding of the experience of her pre-adolescent daughter. It requires more than methods and techniques to cope with a rebelling son who doesn't know himself why he resents the direction of his mother or the stern authority of his father. Insight and understanding help, so do patience and affection, and in some cases only time will provide the solution.

In building a reasonable scheme of discipline, there are some basic considerations which must be taken into account. The adult either makes these judgments after adequate thought or slips into taking a position without realizing it. These considerations concern (1) the nature of the child, (2) the nature of the child's world, (3) the goals of child rearing, and (4) the context in which the discipline operates.

THE NATURE OF THE CHILD

Human nature is a puzzle. Are human beings naturally good, naturally bad, or neither? Our answer to this question will influence how we plan and operate our scheme of discipline. If we consider the child naturally bad, we will be tempted to emphasize the use of restrictions, rigid control, and harsh punishment. If we consider the child naturally good, we will tend to emphasize free expression and discard controls and direction. However, the safest and soundest approach is to consider the child neither good nor bad by nature but a bundle of potentialities that will become good or bad or a mixture of both in terms of how he is treated, the kinds of experiences he has, and what he learns.

The adjectives parents use to describe their children reveal something of their underlying attitudes. Disobedient, stubborn, naughty, bad, little monster are just a few of the words parents have used in telling me about their children. They reflect a punitive rather than what could be called an educative approach. The punitive approach assumes that the child is bad and must be coerced into goodness; every indication of immaturity or misbehaviour must be punished. The child must be made to suffer for his badness. The most serious sin is disobedience. If the parent spares the rod the child will become "set" in his bad ways. This is the negative, punitive approach.

In contrast to this is the positive, educative approach based on acceptance of the child as he is, an immature, learning individual. He is not good or bad; he behaves the way he does because of a complex of impulses, desires, and wants and because of what he has learned or failed to learn. The adult's role is that of guiding this learning and helping the child to channel his drives and wants into desirable forms of expression. The adult must direct, guide, and even restrict the behaviour of young children.

Another aspect of the nature of the child that deserves comment is his heredity and how much weight is to be given to hereditary factors. We are aware that heredity lays the foundation for development, helps to determine the basic structure and thus provides the potentialities and limitations of the individual's development. However, we are also sure that most of the important aspects of personality and character are the result of the treatment the child receives, the experiences he has, and the lessons he learns or fails to learn. With full awareness of the importance of heredity, we put our emphasis on training and environmental influences. Once the child is conceived there is little or nothing we can do about heredity but much we can do to see that the right kind of environmental influences are provided.

The most important characteristic of human nature is flexibility – modifiability or learning potential. The child is naturally a learner. Every experience leaves him a slightly different person, for every experience influences to some extent subsequent activity. For this reason all our dealings have a twofold significance, one that affects the present situation and one that affects personality and character.

THE CHILD'S WORLD

The child is born into a structured society with a complex set of customs, mores, rules, and laws. Because the child is a member of the family and will become a member of many other groups, he will never be able to do as he likes. He will always be subject to the demands and restrictions of the groups of which he is a member. Freedom, in the sense of doing whatever he likes, will never be possible for him. However, freedom coupled with responsibility, is his birthright. Our plan of discipline, then, should be designed to help him to acquire the responsibility that makes freedom meaningful and possible.

The child's environment not only makes demands on him and imposes restrictions on his activity but can provide opportunities for satisfying activity, learning, and self-fulfilment. A reasonable scheme of discipline will make sure that such opportunities are rich and varied. In fact, the mark of such discipline is this positive emphasis.

The child's world is far from perfect. This poses the problem of whether we should train the child to conform with this imperfect society or whether we should help him to participate in its improvement. Conforming must not be considered a virtue, but conformity to the necessary central core of society's rules is a plain necessity. Discipline will include chances to develop an understanding of these rules and to build an individual pattern of taste and preference. The child's conformity and also his non-conformity will have a rational basis.

GOALS OF DISCIPLINE

Discipline has two main goals which might be called immediate and long-range. The immediate goal is the control and direction of the child so that he may enjoy the greatest possible satisfaction from the present situation without hindering or interfering with other people. The long-range goal, on the other hand, is the personality and character development of the child resulting in a self-disciplined adult. These goals are not necessarily incompatible. It should be possible to exercise the necessary controls in such a way as to contribute to the long-term development of the child. The adult, then, has a double purpose in supervising and guiding the child's behaviour; to take care of the present situation and to help move the child nearer to a condition where he no longer needs control and guidance. The best kind of control is that which eventually makes external control unnecessary. For example, one of the easiest forms of control is bribery, offering rewards for "good" behaviour. It works. You can get a child to do almost anything within his ability if you make the bribe attractive enough, but by so doing you will also help the child to learn to evaluate activity mainly in terms of what he gets, in other words "what's in it for me?" Rewards may be worthwhile in terms of immediate results but quite undesirable in long-range results. The problem can be simply stated even though the solution is complex and difficult: to so direct, motivate, and control the child as to take care of the present situation and to achieve the desired effect on his learning.

Discipline is also shaped by the values emphasized by the adult. The adult, for instance, may give a high value to obedience, which to him means doing what you are told without question. Obedience becomes an end in itself, a virtue to be cultivated. The child who is well trained to obey in this manner may lose some of his individuality, initiative, and creativity – a rather high price to pay for the comfort of the adult.

The values of the adult will determine the kinds of behaviour he approves and disapproves. These values will colour all his efforts to control the child. The methods and techniques used will not be as important as how the techniques are used.

CONTEXT OF DISCIPLINE

Even though such terms as "atmosphere of the home" and "environmental climate" are rather vague and difficult to define, they do hold the clue to effective discipline. The individual event and the way in which the adult tries to control the child are not so important as the total picture, the relationship between the child and the adult and the whole context in which the discipline is functioning. Two adults using precisely the same methods will obtain very different results because the contexts are different. The most important aspects of the context of discipline are affection, acceptance, and support. Children not only thrive in this kind of atmosphere but the necessary controls, restrictions, and directions are much more effective. Children welcome guidance and direction when they feel accepted, wanted, and respected by the adult.

PROGRESSIVE NATURE OF DISCIPLINE

The infant is incapable of choice, self-regulation, or control and all decisions, directions, and regulation must come from the adult. Eighteen or twenty years later, we hope that the individual will be able to manage his own affairs adequately and will no longer need external control. In the years between infancy and maturity there must be external control while self-discipline is being learned. Experience shows that the best way to produce a self-disciplined adult is to start early to provide chances to practice self-management, make choices, and be responsible. Thus, in the pre-school years, the school-age period, and in adolescence the child can be given increasing opportunities to practice self-discipline. Every year should see more and more areas in which the child is given increased responsibility and freedom. The pattern of discipline changes progressively as the child learns and becomes more mature and responsible. This process cannot be hurried; it must be gradual. On the other hand, the child's progress towards self-discipline can be hindered if he is too protected or if the external control is too complete and does not allow for choices and practice in self-management.

REQUIREMENTS

Planned requirements, that is, necessary rules and regulations, the things the child must and must not do, are essential. Some of the principles to guide this planning are the following. Requirements should be at a minimum and should include only those that are necessary for the welfare of the child or the functioning of the group. They should be situational, that is, required by the situation, not by the whim of the adult. They should be consistent, the same situation always having the same requirement. They should be within the capacity of the child and they should be understood by him. In short they should be reasonable.

Children need limits. They must be protected from danger. This can be ensured partly by arranging the environment; for example, by building fences and locking medicine cabinets. When all sensible precautions have been taken, there will still be need for controls, rules, and must-nots. Other people must be protected from the impulsive, immature, ignorant child while he is learning how to behave towards others. Even though furniture and possessions are not as important as people, there is no reason why the child should be allowed to destroy or damage the valued possessions of the home or community. Children need limits for their own security, and this feeling is enhanced when their adults protect them from their own destructiveness.

Security springs partly from order, regularity, and consistent requirements. In fact, young children seem to seek order and regularity and give every indication of being happy when they can depend on a certain amount of it in their world. Part of this order is based on planned, reasonable requirements, both positive and negative.

REQUIREMENTS ENFORCED BY CONSEQUENCES

Rules and requirements have very little meaning unless there is some method of enforcing them. Enforcing requirements can be seen in the larger context of consequences, that is, we can think of all behaviour as having consequences. We can also state that intelligent choices and decisions are made by anticipating consequences and directing behaviour in these terms.

There are two kinds of consequences, natural and arbitrary. Although natural consequences are usually consistent, they are not always immediate and sometimes they are drastic. Arbitrary consequences are arranged, added, and deliberate. If arbitrary consequences are to be helpful they should be as consistent as possible, immediate, invariable, and logically related to the behaviour.

Consequences following desirable behaviour are just as important as consequences following undesirable behaviour. The natural consequences of desirable activity are feelings of success, adequacy, and achievement. Arbitrary consequences include social approval, notations of success, and tangible rewards. These arbitrary consequences should be used with care as it is very easy for the child to learn to work for them, thus obscuring the value of the activity itself.

Virtue is its own reward is another way of saying that adequate behaviour carries its own intrinsic consequence of satisfaction. The use of rewards seems to be an admission that the activity is not worthwhile in itself and that something must be added to make it so. Pay for good behaviour simply means that the child is learning to behave as someone else wants him to, for a price. The reward can very easily become more important than the behaviour itself. Rewards nearly always lead to barter. The child soon learns to bargain and the price of goodness can be raised. Rewards can be bribes and as such are based on the false idea that if we can induce the child to do something often enough a habit will be formed and the bribe will then not be needed. This is not the way it works. The child learns what he practices; when he practices working for a reward he learns the reward habit, not the habit of tidiness, punctuality, neatness, or whatever the adult has in mind.

Consequences for undesirable behaviour follow the same kind of pattern. The natural consequences are feelings of failure, inadequacy, and falling short of what is desirable, whereas the arbitrary consequences are social disapproval expressed in a variety of ways, punishments of various kinds, deprivation of materials, experiences and privileges, and isolation. Punishment is the least desirable consequence because it generates resentment, rationalization, and rebellion. Any of the arbitrary consequences can become punitive, depending on how they are used. For instance, isolation can be a punishment if there is a suggestion of blame and recrimination. However, isolation can be used in an educational way. Whether it is punitive or educative depends on the attitude of the adult who administers it.

Discipline need not be punishment and consequences need not be punitive. Of course, it is difficult for the parent not to assume a punitive attitude towards the child at times. Children can be very irritating and everyone's patience has limits. Occasional loss of patience and even physical abuse can be accepted by the child. It may help him to see that even his loving parents, like himself, have angry and hostile feelings. A steady diet of punishment, however, cannot form the core of an adequate scheme of discipline. It shuts the child out of the adult's world: it means rejection and erects barriers between the child and the adult which are very difficult to remove. It is the enemy of respect, trust, and confidence.

Although it may seem impossible, a parent can be annoyed and even angry about a broken vase or a scratch on a treasured table, and yet not be punitive towards the child. This is akin to disapproval of an act without disapproval of the person. It is a difficult but effective mental gymnastic.

In administering consequences the most important features are consistency and feeling. The more consistent the consequences, the easier and sooner the child learns. The most effective feeling aspect is a non-punitive, reasonable one, so that the child does not think of the consequences as personal retaliation but rather as the result of his own behaviour.

A positive, non-punitive discipline is a plan of training which does not neglect control and yet maintains a relationship of respect, acceptance, and affection. The kind of control used is based on the authority of a person whose wisdom the child respects because he is just, honest, understanding, and loving. Is this too much to expect of parents? It asks a lot but it pays big dividends.

This positive discipline leans heavily on indirect control or the power of an interesting, varied environment which provides opportunities for satisfying activities. The actual occasions of direct control are reduced when there is adequate environmental control. Here an atmosphere of acceptance and affection and an attitude of expecting the best from the child play a part. This is what the permissive attitude can be when it functions in a framework of reasonable direction and necessary limitation.

PRACTICAL SUGGESTIONS

By way of conclusion, a number of suggestions are offered. These are not rules but rather abbreviated statements of important aspects of discipline.

1 Study the child to learn what you can expect so that you can take into account his present ability and stage of development.
2 Treat the child with respect and consideration. Try to understand the child's motives and point of view. Avoid showing off the child, discussing him in his hearing, comparing him with other children, and any form of criticism or belittling.

3 Always keep faith with the child; deal with him honestly and truthfully. Keep promises and never use threats.

4 Plan the requirements carefully, keeping them to a minimum and enforcing them consistently.

5 Emphasize positive direction, use re-direction rather than inhibition.

6 Stress an accepting, affectionate attitude so that the child can feel wanted and loved.

7 Provide plenty of opportunities for real choices and chances for the practice of self-direction.

8 Build increasing opportunities for the child to feel that he is an important member of the family by sharing family work, responsibilities, discussions, and planning.

9 Provide opportunities for interesting wholesome activities – space, time, materials, ideas, and companions for free play.

10 Never lose faith in the child, let him feel your trust and confidence in him no matter how he behaves.

11 Strive for a non-punitive approach. Eliminate the blame, recrimination, and emotion of punishment. Think of ways to help the child to learn rather than ways to make him suffer.

Discipline and education[5]

Any philosophy of discipline should have as its goal the development of the child into a secure, mentally healthy, and productive adult. The purpose of this section is to look at a number of questions relating to education in the light of the philosophy of discipline advanced in the previous pages of this chapter.

Two goals have traditionally been dominant in elementary education: (1) the mastery of subject matter (knowledge) and (2) the development of skills (reading, writing). There is no question that certain fundamental knowledge is necessary (although there may be some question as to what is fundamental) and that some skills such as reading and writing are essential in our society. However, by placing the emphasis here, a broader and more important goal of education, that of the development of a disciplined approach to learning tends to become forgotten. It is partly because of this misplaced emphasis that so many gifted chil-

5 D. K. Bernhardt, "The philosophy of discipline and education," *Bull. Inst. Child Stud.*, 1963, 23(4), 5–8.

dren get bored with school and therefore their great potential is lost to themselves and to society.

Much of what is taught at school is soon forgotten. This is not necessarily a matter for concern since much of what is taught need not be part of the child's (and later the adult's) immediate recall. This fact does emphasize, however, that the important goal should be the development in the pupil of a disciplined approach to learning, a persistent striving towards meaningful goals at no matter what intellectual level the child is operating. Especially in the early years, it is the approach, not the material, which is most important. The development of such an approach makes it possible for children of moderate intellectual abilities sometimes to surpass children of higher intellectual abilities.

Let us consider how the development of this disciplined approach may be fostered in the child. Whitehead (1923, p. 42) said: "There can be no mental development without interest. Interest is the *sine qua non* for attention and apprehension." Individuals do not learn only in school. They are continually learning, but this learning usually takes place in areas and activities which interest them. Here a circular process sets in; the more a person learns in an area the more interested he is likely to become in that area and consequently the more he learns.

The most important factor here is the development by the child of an inner motivation to learn which will energize this disciplined approach. How does this come about? Where do the familiar rewards and punishments fit into this motivation picture? As pointed out earlier in this chapter, because we like rewards, and because the reward technique seems to yield immediate results, there is a temptation to bribe children. The use of rewards often brings immediate results (better grades, for example), but these immediate results tend to obscure the long-range goals, especially the goal of a disciplined approach to learning. Inner motivation is not developed and later, in the absence of these rewards, the child is not able to motivate himself. Furthermore, the use of bribes can have a harmful effect on the attitudes and emotions of the child.

There are other problems associated with the use of a reward system. Often the rewards are so unattainable that only a few can realistically aspire to them. The others become discouraged. Everyone cannot hope to be first in the class or on the school honour roll. Too great an emphasis on a reward system can lead to too much deference to authority (the teachers and parents) and this, in turn, can lead to stereotyped behaviour on the part of the child, which stifles originality and creativity.

This is not to say, however, that all rewards are bad. For healthy development and learning the child needs constant encouragement and praise meaningfully given for actual accomplishments, no matter how small they may be. We hope that the child will gradually develop a reward or motivational system within himself, but there will always be a place for recognizing his accomplishments and his worth as an individual.

If there is little room for the traditional reward system in the development of a disciplined approach to learning, there is even less room for the traditional punishment system. Punishment interferes with the interpersonal relationship of teacher and pupil, lowers the mental health level of the individual, and often reinforces the behaviour punished. As Laycock (1954, p. 88) states: "Punishment says 'stop it' but does not tell what to do."

Competition is a variation of the reward and punishment system in the school. It is obvious that, for some children, competition in school often brings visible desirable results. Certainly it is true that much of our society is founded on competition and that there must be a place for it in the child's development pattern to keep him from being overwhelmed by it later. However, this can be provided outside the academic situation in athletic and intellectual games. Here the teams or individuals can be evenly paired with team effort and organization leading to success.

Competitiveness appears to be on the increase in the school system, probably because of the increased value being placed on education and the concomitant increasing difficulty in getting into college. However, especially at the lower levels of education, where it is necessary to lay the proper foundation for the approach to learning, competition can be very damaging. Pupils who are forced to compete for favourable evaluations may develop extraneous motives for learning and the disciplined approach which is so important for future development becomes lost in the shuffle. In addition, it compels the weak students to compete with the stronger ones.

A related, highly complicated question is that of failure. It is true that failure can be used to spur the pupil on to greater endeavour, but continued failure is devastating to the child and this is often found in the schools. As Laycock (1954) points out, in life situations a man who has failed at his job does not continue at that job, but in the schools the pupil is often required to continue a task at which he has continually failed.

Can a school abandon the threat of failure without ruining the child's incentives? There are, of course, some children who need special programmes because of lower abilities or emotional problems. Failure is not going to solve this situation. For the others there is no reason why failure needs to be held over their heads if the proper approach to learning is started early in the child's life. In most cases non-promotion of pupils in order to assure mastery of subject matter in typical lock-step elementary school grades does not seem to accomplish this objective. Furthermore, failure of this kind can turn the pupil against the school and against academic learning and be highly detrimental to the development of the kind of approach that has been discussed here.

However, promotion into a higher grade of someone who is not yet ready for it can be very frustrating especially in the traditional lock-step classroom. A more flexible approach can help to solve this difficulty. Adaptable grouping for the various subjects or units within the class allows the child more freedom to work at his own rate. For evaluation purposes the emphasis should be on a comparison of the child's present work with his past work and also with an absolute scale which indicates where he is now and where he should be going next. Modern teaching machines illustrate the application of these two ideas for they exclude failure: the child works along at his own rate until he has finished the unit, at which time he starts another. The only indication of individual differences in the well worked out teaching machine unit is in the rate of progression.

Finally, then, it becomes clear that, instead of developing the child's motivation through these negative factors or through bribes it is important to develop intrinsic motives within the child – the feeling of satisfaction for a job well done. The extrinsic motives, like rewards, do not establish satisfaction for the pupil in what should be his real goals – the satisfactory learning of skills and knowledge. It is the ability and desire for sustained effort towards a meaningful goal that must be developed and developed early. This can be accomplished (1) by arousal of interest in the pupil, along with a recognition of the consequences, (2) through the development of appropriate tasks, and (3) through the patient and consistent efforts of the teacher and the parents to show genuine interest in the child's work and in his worth as an individual.

REFERENCES

B. Bettelheim, *Truants from life* (Glencoe: Free Press of Glencoe, 1955).
S. R. Laycock, *Teaching and Learning* (Toronto: Copp Clark, 1954).
A. N. Whitehead, "The rhythmic claims of freedom and discipline," 1923. Reprinted in *The aims of education and other essays* (New York: Mentor, 1949).

Chapter 7

Discipline Problems

Any philosophy of discipline will seem impressive when everything is going well. It is, however, when the pattern breaks down and the children misbehave that the parents and the philosophy are tested.

The articles in this chapter outline the necessity of routines and consistency and then discuss what parents should and should not do at difficult times, mealtime and bedtime, for example. Such problems as breaking annoying habits, sibling rivalry, and the submissive child are also examined.

Routines for the young child[1]

One of the most important problems for the parents of an infant is the establishment of a routine. There are at least three possibilities: (1) have no established routine at all; (2) adopt a ready-made schedule and force or try to force the child to conform to it; (3) build a routine that is suitable to the individual child. Of these three possibilities, the third seems to us the most reasonable.

The first possibility – no established routine – has been advocated as a method of letting a wise nature decide. The child is fed when he hollers for it or whenever it occurs to the parent to do so. He is put to bed when it is most convenient. To me such lack of regularity and order looks like chaos and confusion and to the infant I am sure it seems like neglect and insecurity. The infant or young child without a regular routine must be confused and insecure, for he has little in his world that is dependable and stable. No established routine usually means that the parents haven't taken the time to do the necessary planning.

The second possibility – a ready-made routine and forcing the child to conform – is undesirable because of the great individual differences that exist among children. Although all infants need food, they do not all need the same amount, and although they all need sleep the amount required by one child may vary considerably from that required by another. A ready-made routine, then, is not as good as an individually determined routine. No two children are exactly alike and they should not be expected to behave alike.

For the infant a tailored-to-measure routine is best, but as he grows

1 K. S. Bernhardt, "Routines for the young child," *Parent Educ. Bull.*, 1946, no. 37, 1 – 3.

older he must learn to conform to the customs of the society in which he is to live. Thus, the individually patterned routine must be changed gradually to one that fits into the family and community pattern.

How is a good routine for the infant determined? The infant has an unmistakable language. His behaviour mirrors his wants and feelings. His needs for sleep, food, activity, and comfort are signalled by his behaviour, especially his vocal behaviour. True, he has no words to use but his withdrawal and rejection and his approach and acceptance of situations speak loudly to the observant parent. His cries of distress and hunger eloquently describe how he feels, and his happy cooing and relaxed condition tell their story of comfort and well-being. These are the signs that can be used by the parent to determine the pattern of the infant's routine. We can know when he is hungry, sleepy, comfortable or uncomfortable and on the basis of this knowledge we can build for him a schedule of care which suits his own particular needs and rhythm. A fairly regular schedule is necessary: (1) because it provides a basis for his feeling of security, (2) because it aids learning, and (3) because it helps to deal with the many distractions which hinder the easy, business-like satisfaction of basic needs.

The infant can learn to conform to a regular schedule and it is to his advantage to do so. The early years are important because what happens then determines the developments which will play a large part in his smooth adjustment to life. The foundations of character and personality are laid in these early experiences. A little care and planning at the beginning will pay large dividends later.

When a routine has been established for the baby, with regular feeding times, sleeping times and so on, and if this routine is realistic in terms of the expressed needs and rhythm of the child, a splendid start has been made. But it is only a beginning because the child does not stand still. He is growing, maturing, and learning and with this growth and development there come changes in his needs and wants. A good routine must keep pace with his development. Feeding times become less frequent, the pattern of sleep and wakefulness changes, and the day's schedule must change too. The changes should not, however, be too sudden. The kind of careful observation that went into the determination of the original routine is needed for its subsequent modification. An observant parent can tell when the child is ready for a change.

It is a common mistake to use the age of the child as a guide to the modification of his routine. It is the child's own development rhythm that should determine the changes and not his actual age, since children vary greatly in their rate of development.

As we have said, the individually determined schedule for the infant is gradually and progressively changed into a routine that fits the pattern of society. When this transition is complete the routine is such that it fits the family and community pattern. At the beginning the main and almost the only consideration was the child's own needs; later, other features such as the convenience of the family group and the demands of social living must be taken into consideration. Now the child must learn to conform and to satisfy his needs in a socially acceptable manner. This transition takes time and should be gradual.

As the child's understanding increases he can and should learn that there are things that he must do whether he wants to or not. He learns that living includes compulsions and necessities and that he can have more fun and happiness when he shapes his behaviour to fit the dictates of society and not merely his own desires. This learning can begin when the infant becomes a toddler. Up to this time he has been almost completely dependent on others. Now he can move around for himself and is thus less dependent. Because there is now a greater chance of his getting into trouble or danger, there must be regulation and control.

It is in the daily routines that the toddler can best learn to conform to the necessary requirements of living. So his routine becomes to some extent arbitrary. Regular meal hours, set times for sleep, a regular toilet routine, and set times for play are scheduled, but now this schedule may not exactly fit his needs and he must learn that there is a time for one kind of behaviour and another time for a different behaviour. He is beginning to learn that living makes demands on him and that there are considerations other than his own feelings.

A regular routine removes these features from the realm of parents' whims. The child learns, for instance that he goes to bed not just when the parent thinks of it but at a regular time. Therefore, there should be no exceptions to routines, because exceptions are the material out of which problems and difficulties are made. Once a child has learned that he can evade a routine he will try almost anything to get out of it when he wants to do something else. The simplest solution is to make sure that there are no exceptions. Even if he coaxes or throws a temper tantrum he still has the routine to carry through when he has recovered.

There is no reason why the child shouldn't enjoy the routine activities, but they should not be made to look like play. The routine is business, serious business that must be carried through. It is a job to be done. Eating, sleeping, dressing, washing, toilet and other such routines should be made pleasant for the child but nevertheless, situations in which a certain kind of behaviour, is required and to which he must conform. It is important also not to insist on non-essentials and thus make the child's life too regimented and managed. Along with the routines there are play activities – things that the child can do or not do as he likes.

The child is helped to conform when the situation is planned carefully and the requirements are made clear and understandable. The directions should be simple, positive, and within his ability to understand. His attention is directed to the business at hand. Distractions and confusion are avoided. He is given assistance when he needs it but not so much that the activity is done for him. He receives encouragement and a word of praise when he conforms and does his best.

The attitude of the adult in routine situations should be unemotional and impersonal but interested. It is made clear that it is the child's responsibility not the parent's. In general toddlers like to conform. They usually accept routines as a matter of course, waste very little time, and get them finished so that they can get back to play. They are happier and more secure when they know what they can expect and depend on. When the child rebels against a routine we can be sure that we haven't managed the situation very well, that we haven't made it clear that it is a requirement, or that we have tried to hurry the child beyond his ability to perform.

Annoying habits[2]

All children are a nuisance some of the time and it is a very exceptional parent who does not occasionally lose patience. In the hundred and one situations of everyday life in the family there are many times when the behaviour of the young child can be annoying. He will dawdle, play with his food, spill his milk, make a mess with paste or paints, leave his play materials lying around, be too noisy, get under foot, bump into furniture, interrupt conversation, forget to do what is required of him, fail to hang up his towel, leave the wash basin in a mess, and perform dozens of other equally irritating childish acts. In other words, children will persist in being childish because, after all, they are children.

We have all noticed that children are especially provoking when we are tired or worried or busy. Later, when we are calmer and less hur-

2 K. S. Bernhardt, "Annoying habits," in *Living with children*, no. 3, 1958, Tangley Oaks Educational Center.

ried, we realize that part of the reason for our annoyance was not so much what the child did or failed to do but our own condition. Sometimes, also, we realize that a little planning on our part would lessen the provoking aspects of children's behaviour. The following suggestions should be helpful in reducing the number of times a day young children tax the patience of their parents.

1 Know what you can reasonably expect from your children. Many of our annoyances arise from expecting the impossible. To expect an active young child to sit still without wriggling, interrupting adult conversation, or fiddling with things is expecting the impossible. It is better to give him something to play with so he can be active in less annoying ways.

2 Make it easy for the child to conform. Low pegs for his clothes, a convenient place for him to keep his play materials, a place for play, his towel fastened to the rack are but a few examples of arranging the child's environment so that it is easier for him to do what is desired.

3 Making commands less personal helps to get results. For instance, instead of "Mother wants you to go to bed," the simple formula "It is now bedtime" seems to be easier for the child to accept and carry out.

4 Dawdling, one of the most common annoyances, is often the result of the parent trying to hurry the child. The more the parent tries to hurry the child the more he slows down. He often enjoys the experience of being the centre of attention and even the display of adult impatience. Setting a reasonable time limit for the meal or dressing or similar activities helps. Some parents have found that the kitchen timer comes in handy. It can be set to ring in fifteen or twenty minutes as a signal that the meal is over. If the child can tell time by the clock it is possible to let that impersonal gadget do the nagging.

5 Having a fairly regular routine removes some of the confusion for the child and some of the annoyances for the parent. This routine for the young child can include a time for play, a time for rest, a time for bed, a time for the bath, a time for a story or to watch TV, and even a time for being the centre of attention. When the child knows that these various parts of the day will come around at a fairly dependable time he does not have to keep bothering Mother.

6 Being alert to signs of fatigue and boredom and being prepared with re-direction can avoid a great many irritations. This means occasionally providing something new in the way of play materials or suggesting new ideas. This is very important on those difficult days of convalescence from illness or when rain keeps the child inside.

7 A rest from constant supervision usually puts Mother into a frame of mind that enables her to carry on without being so frequently provoked. Father (or someone else) can take over for awhile.

8 Perhaps the most important suggestion of all is to decide what is important and must be enforced and deliberately to let the less essential things go for the time being. When we try to do too much in the way of regulating the young child's behaviour and insist on too much we usually find ourselves losing patience and being provoked by little things that are not very important. A few requirements, clearly stated and easily understood by the child, can and should be enforced consistently.

We have to keep reminding ourselves that the attention span of the young child is short, that he is very easily distracted, that he is sure to forget some things, that his skills are still imperfect, and that he will learn eventually to do things better, to become more capable and less provoking if we give him the time and opportunity for such learning. In all this, our attitudes and example are very important. It is a sobering thought to remember that some of the child's irritating patterns of behaviour have been picked up from us. Children are great imitators: they absorb many of their behaviour patterns from watching other people. Cheerfulness, consideration for others, being responsible, and other attitudes are catching. So are whining, complaining, and being annoyed.

Bringing up children is a mixed experience. It has many exciting, satisfying aspects, but there are sure to be many irritating features as well. Perhaps if we can emphasize the pleasing features, the less pleasant will not be too apparent. As parents we must pay attention to those things in the child's behaviour which may be serious; the many small but irritating features of the day's activities, which are in many cases but passing phases of development, can be safely overlooked.

Making and breaking habits[3]

We parents have two main responsibilities. One is to wholeheartedly accept our children so that they can feel wanted, loved, and secure in their world. The other is to guide and direct their learning. Thus child

3 K. S. Bernhardt, "Making and breaking habits," in *Living with children*, no. 3.

rearing means creating an atmosphere of love, acceptance, and security and then in this context arranging for the kind of learning that is necessary for the child to become a self-disciplined adult. It is this second parental responsibility with which we are concerned here.

The child is by nature a learner. He is, in fact, learning all the time. Every experience he has teaches him something. Our job, then, is not to get him to learn or to stop him from learning but to make sure that the conditions are right for the most desirable kinds of learning.

The habits the child acquires will depend on the results of his activities. When his behaviour succeeds in getting him what he wants, that form of behaviour will tend to persist. The activity which leads to unpleasant or undesired consequences tends to disappear. Part, at least, of the guidance of learning is making sure that the right consequences happen as a result of the child's efforts.

Learning readiness is also important. The child can learn only those things for which his growth and development have made him ready. It is useless, for instance, to try to get the infant to learn to control his bladder until he is old enough to be able to control the muscles concerned and to recognize the sensations of a full bladder. Efforts to have him learn before he is ready for it can only result in unhealthy strains and tensions. There is an optimum time for most learning. The child's behaviour will indicate to an observant parent when he is ready to learn to feed himself, to manage his dressing and washing, to acquire the many skills of everyday life. He will probably not be ready for the complex learning involved in social play much before his second birthday, and reading readiness will not be apparent much before he is six. It should be stressed, however, that we need to be alert to any signs of learning readiness so that we can provide the opportunities at the right time.

The amount of help and "teaching" necessary for learning is usually less than most of us think. We can actually hinder learning by doing too much for the child. He has to do a certain amount of struggling on his own in order to acquire most skills. What we have to decide is when our help and direction is necessary to get the child over the discouraging parts of the activity. It we step in too soon or too often the child easily learns to depend on outside help and will not try enough for himself. He has to make some mistakes. He can learn to feed himself, for instance, only by doing a certain amount of spilling. It is always a temptation for adults to blame and scold or punish the child for his mistakes, and some children become afraid to try. We accept most mistakes for what they are, parts of the process of learning.

It is almost inevitable that the child will acquire some habits that are undesirable and so we are faced with the challenging task of re-education. Perhaps instead of thinking of this as "breaking habits," it would be better if we thought of it as re-learning or substitute learning. Actually, it is almost impossible to "break" or stop an habitual activity, but it is usually possible to redirect it. This is the key to what is usually called breaking habits. Experience has shown that attempts to break habits are usually unsuccessful whereas redirection or substitution is almost always successful. For example, many parents have struggled hard to break their children of the habit of sucking their thumbs, of biting their nails, of using slang, of tracking mud into the house, of dozens of other such "bad" habits. In most cases their efforts have been relatively unsuccessful. In some cases the child has dropped the habit because something else has become more important to him. When parents arrange for other activities to take the place of the undesirable ones they encounter relatively little difficulty. What has been called "breaking habits" should be thought of in much the same terms as any learning, for that is what it is, learning to do something different.

Sometimes so-called bad habits in children are nothing more than the natural behaviour at that stage of development. For instance, the young child who wiggles in his chair instead of sitting still, the boy who fiddles with the silverware at the dinner table, the child who interrupts conversations, and literally hundreds of similar behaviour patterns are only phases of the child's immaturity which will disappear spontaneously.

There are other "bad" habits in children that are simply the child's imitation of his parents or other persons. If Mother resorts to slapping to solve problems, it is not surprising to find the child using the same method with his playmates. If parents yell at their children, we can be almost sure that the child will learn to yell back.

It can be an exciting experience for the parent to watch the day-by-day learning of his children; but he can do more than watch, he can take part in the process himself. Indeed, it is his responsibility to do so. The adult's part lies mainly in the provision of the opportunities for learning; he cannot do the actual learning. This providing of opportunities includes arranging the stage, providing the materials, setting a good example, giving commendation when needed, and re-directing on occasion. We must beware of trying to hurry the child, expecting too much too soon, or providing tasks beyond his present ability.

Anti-social acts [4]

Anti-social behaviour can be defined as behaviour in which the child, although knowing better, violates the rules or standards of the group, family, school, or community. This does not include the immature behaviour of the young child which stems from his ignorance of what society requires of its members, nor the nuisance behaviour of children which may be annoying but not anti-social in the sense of breaking rules and deliberately disobeying the demands of the group.

Anti-social behaviour cannot be accounted for in such simple terms as naughtiness, stubbornness, or disobedience. We have to get behind these labels and try to discover the real cause. We must also be careful not to blame the child for behaviour which, although undesirable, may be caused by requirements that are impossible for him to fulfil.

We expect the child to learn that living in any group such as the family and being a member of a team or a classroom group or a community means that he can not always do as he likes. Social groups, in order to function, must have rules and restrictions. Anti-social behaviour against these rules violates the restrictions. Rules, however, are more easily accepted and followed when they are understood and appear both necessary and sensible. Consequently, one phase of this problem is helping the child to know what the rules are and why they are necessary. This can be done to some extent by having the child participate in making the rules. He can then see that the rule is not just a whim of a parent or teacher but a sensible regulation designed to allow everybody to have more fun and to get more out of the situation.

If the child understands a rule and still fails to conform, there is always some reason for it. Our job as adults is to try to find out why the child behaves that way so that we can help him to learn. Simple punishment, therefore, is rarely adequate in dealing with non-conformity. Every non-conformity should bring a consequence. For example, if the child does not behave in an acceptable way at the family dinner table, as a consequence he should eat by himself until he is ready to behave in an acceptable way. The child who persists in leaving his play materials lying around instead of putting them away should be deprived of

4 K. S. Bernhardt, "Anti-social acts," in *Living with children*, no. 2.

their use to help him learn to abide by the sensible rule of putting them away. If property is destroyed the child should help make good the damage. In other words, all anti-social behaviour should bring a consequence which the child can recognize as the direct result of his behaviour.

However, there are some cases of anti-social behaviour that require more than simple consequences for their cure. These are the cases where the child's behaviour has some deeper meaning than just forgetfulness or carelessness. For example, the child destroys things, or steals, or lies as an expression of his resentment against his parents or others, or because he is jealous, or afraid, or insecure. The simple consequence should follow but the parent needs to investigate further to discover the underlying cause of the behaviour. Only when a parent does this is he able to be helpful in the long run.

Sometimes the basic cause of anti-social behaviour is to be found in our treatment of the child. He may feel that we are unfair, that we require of him unreasonable things, that we do not understand him, that we do not want him. If any of these feelings are involved, it is important that we take steps to rectify them; otherwise no amount of punishment or use of consequences will serve.

When dealing with anti-social behaviour we must recognize that there are hundreds of possible reasons for it. A child may feel rejected by either parents or playmates. He may be trying to protect himself against punishment or over-strict discipline. He may steal or lie to get attention or to try to keep up with his companions. He may feel unimportant at school or at home. He may be compensating for physical or intellectual difficulties either real or imagined. He may have been spoiled earlier and now have the feeling that he should be allowed to do as he likes. In any case it is necessary to remember that the child is not inherently bad and that if he has sufficient opportunities to satisfy his desires in acceptable ways he will not have to resort to anti-social behaviour. There is nothing to be gained by blaming the child and labelling him bad. In fact, it is a mistake. However, this does not mean that we condone the undesirable behaviour. Our job is to help the child learn how to behave in a civilized way. This takes time and the child will make many errors along the way. He needs to feel that we are with him, on his side, that we do not love him any less even when his behaviour is at its worst. We have the difficult job of re-educating the child without building resentments and enmity.

Expectation is a most effective factor. We get from children about what we expect. When we expect them to conform to sensible, reasonable requirements they usually do so. When we expect them to give trouble they rarely disappoint us. This stems from the fact that one of the most important aspects of child training is an attitude of trust and confidence in the child. Give a dog (or a child) a bad name and he will try to live up to it. It works the other way, too.

The child's manners, morals, and general attitudes to life are largely the product of two things, the kind of example he has to follow and the kind of treatment he receives. Morals are more caught than taught. The mother who keeps saying to her daughter, "You should always tell the truth, only bad little girls tell lies" can easily nullify this teaching by telling her to answer the door and if it is Mrs. Jones "tell her I'm not at home." And Father may not be helping the moral development of his son when he tells him to keep a sharp lookout in the back window of the car for the traffic policeman. Children learn more through these little daily incidents than from all the deliberate attempts to teach them to do right.

The submissive child[5]

A submissive child is one who lacks balance because he has learned to follow, conform, and obey others but has not learned to lead, initiate, or have ideas of his own. There is a place for submission but the submissive child goes further – he is always that way. He has insufficient confidence in himself. He tends to feel inferior and to accept his inferiority without testing himself or trying to overcome it. He is the loser in most situations because he is left out or given inferior roles by his playmates. He is often unhappy and usually quite ineffective.

Healthy social situations are those in which there is a shifting pattern of dominance and submission. The dominant person for the time being is the person with the ideas and skills demanded by the group activity and the submissive persons are those who recognize and accept his leadership. The well-adjusted person socially is one who has learned when to be dominant and when to be submissive, when to be a leader

5 K. S. Bernhardt, "The submissive child," in *Living with children*, no. 1.

and when to follow. His bid for leadership is in terms of bright ideas and relevant skills, and he is content to be a follower when there is someone with more knowledge and skill than himself. No one should try to dominate always, nor should he be content always to submit. So we see that the submissive child is one who has not learned how and when to take the leadership and to gain the co-operation and follower-ship of others.

The submissive child is the timid child, usually afraid of failing, making mistakes, or being laughed at. This is often caused by over-dominant and over-protective parents. When parents demand instant obedience, and provide a pattern of detailed direction of the child's activities, the child while learning his lesson of following commands may fail to learn to think for himself or to plan and manage his own affairs. This child is ill-prepared for situations where initiative and leadership are called for.

Children may become submissive for a variety of reasons. Perhaps foremost among these is domineering parents who, as mentioned above, demand instant obedience. Over-dominant parents can very easily crush the possibilities of leadership, initiative, and creative ability in the child. When this is accompanied by standards so high that the child can rarely achieve them, he can develop feelings of inferiority and timidity which keep him from trying anything new or different. He submits not just to people but also to circumstances and develops a kind of "what's the use?" attitude.

The child might become over-submissive by being subjected to the dominance of an older child in the family or play group, or his sub-missiveness might result from lack of opportunity to follow his own wishes, interests, or ideas. Too much direction and protection may also keep the child from learning that he can achieve things on his own and he thus fails to develop self-confidence and self-assertion. A highly personal type of discipline can have the same result.

Of course, some rules are required for the welfare of the family group and so that the children can learn the necessity for "musts" in life, but these should be kept to a minimum. The child should learn to conform to necessary demands and restrictions, but this conformity should be intelligent, that is, based on understanding rather than fear. It is con-formity based on fear that produces the timid, submissive individual.

There is a time for submission and a time for intelligent aggression. The child who is subjected to a discipline that requires no thought or self-direction seems to learn only to submit. On the other hand, a reasonable discipline that provides chances for legitimate choices and the feeling of managing some things for himself should help the child to move towards self-discipline and thus not be too dependent on control by others.

Sibling rivalry[6]

"Why can't my children play together without this continual bickering?" is a frequent question asked in parent discussion groups. "Is sibling rivalry inevitable? Do brothers and sisters always fight, tell on each other, bicker, argue, tease each other?" One part of the answer to these questions is that although this kind of behaviour is not inevitable it is very common and could be called normal. In other words children (and adults, too) are certainly going to have differences of opinion about things, but siblings (brothers and sisters) have the added feature of competition for parental love and attention. We have come to think of sibling rivalry as a normal aspect of interaction between children in the family. It is only when it is excessive that it becomes a problem. However, there are some things that we parents can do to minimize this rivalry and to help the children to live together without too much bickering, even to enjoy their relationship and benefit from it.

One suggestion is to avoid comparisons of the children as much as possible. Such comparisons are rarely fair and are always undesirable. Differences in age, ability, skill, experience, and interests must be taken into account. In other words all children should be treated as individuals. To say to one child, "Why can't you behave like your sister?" is the same as saying to the child, "You have no right to be different from her." To hold up one child as an example of goodness is to invite other children to resent and dislike him. They may even try to revenge themselves on this paragon. Instead of pitting one child against another we should try to appreciate each child for his own good points, to encourage him to develop his own abilities and to feel important for what he is himself and not just how he compares with the other child. Such an approach should help to minimize sibling rivalry and at the same time

6 K. S. Bernhardt, "Sibling rivalry," in *Living with children*, no. 4.

encourage each child to develop his own individuality as he learns that he is loved for himself and has his own place in the family.

It is also wise to beware of trying to judge or referee children's quarrels or disagreements. In many cases the children can resolve their own differences and settle their own disputes. When we step into the picture, the children, instead of trying to find a solution, concentrate on trying to convince the "judge" that they are right. In other words, it becomes a clear case of sibling rivalry in which they are competing for the parent's approval. When we intervene in favour of one child, the other child almost certainly resents it and feels that it is unfair. When children's disputes and arguments get too strenuous or frequent we can intervene, not to settle the dispute but to suggest other ways of finding a solution or calling off the battle.

Parents sometimes aggravate sibling rivalry by expecting or even requiring brothers and sisters to play together to the exclusion of other children. Sometimes an older brother is told he must let his younger brother "tag along" with him. And sometimes parents insist that children share their treasures with their brothers and sisters. Children can enjoy and get along better with their brothers and sisters if they are not required to be with them most of the time. In other words, each child should be allowed to have his own chosen companions and not be expected to play with his brother or sister just because they happen to belong to the same family. Just because the other child is a brother is no reason why he should be expected to let him misuse treasured play materials. There can be common materials to be shared and used in turn by siblings, but each child should also have the right to own and control some personal belongings.

Occasions for family fun, picnics, excursions, outings, and family parties help to generate a feeling of family unity. Rivalry and competition can be avoided by having the children take turns in suggesting and planning these events. Having fun as a family reduces the frequency and seriousness of sibling quarrels, disputes, and rivalry.

It is difficult for parents to avoid having favourites and showing preferences, but the more we can avoid any signs of such preference or favouritism the more we succeed in minimizing sibling rivalry. Although the handling of more than one child in the family requires the wisdom of Solomon and the patience of Job, our efforts are well repaid by smoother relationships among all members of the family and better personality development for each child.

Make eating a pleasure[7]

The healthy growth and development of the infant and child require good eating habits. Good eating habits do not just happen; they are built by careful planning and intelligent handling of the early food experiences of the young child. One of the commonest complaints that parents bring to child behaviour clinics is that their children show difficulties in eating – food dislikes, dawdling, refusal to eat, playing with the food, among others.

In thinking and planning for good eating habits there are a number of essentials that must be kept in mind: (1) that the child get sufficient amounts and kinds of food, (2) that he enjoy eating, (3) that he learn to eat in a socially acceptable manner, (4) that he eat what is placed before him and not develop food dislikes. These are the objectives to keep in mind in training the child to eat.

We do not intend to give details here about the kinds of food the child should have. There is abundant information available to parents on this subject. It serves our purpose to say that the child must have a well-balanced diet for vigour and growth and protection from infection. As nearly everyone is aware, there are some items that are included in such a diet for both the young child and the adult: milk, eggs, green or yellow vegetables, raw leafy vegetables, whole grain cereals, citrus fruits, and some source of vitamin D.

We are concerned here not so much with what the child eats as with how he eats. As some parents have discovered, they can lead their child to food but they cannot always make him eat. It is quite impossible to provide an adequate, well-balanced diet for the child if you are unable to get some of it past his lips. Many a parent has contemplated the diet list of the paediatrician and has said rather plaintively, "But, Doctor, how do I get him to eat it?"

The eating behaviour of children as well as of adults is controlled largely by hunger and appetite. Hunger is a set of sensations arising from an empty stomach. Appetite on the other hand is the desire for food related to memories of previous satisfying and pleasant experiences of eating. A child can be hungry and have little appetite. This is seen

7 K. S. Bernhardt, "Make eating a pleasure," *Baby News*, 1946, 1(4), 6–7.

in the child who begins a meal eagerly but loses interest in the food after a few mouthfuls. His hunger gets him started but his lack of appetite hinders his continuing. Also, there can be appetite without hunger as, for instance, when the child wants his dessert after a large meal. He is no longer hungry, but he has an appetite for ice cream. In planning, both hunger and appetite must be taken into consideration.

Because hunger supplies such a strong drive, new and unfamiliar foods should be introduced at the beginning of the meal. There is a greater chance of the child accepting the new food when he is hungry and thus combining the pleasure of hunger satisfaction and the acquiring of an appetite for that particular food. The child almost automatically rejects a new flavour, but when he is hungry flavour is less important. New foods should be introduced one at a time, in very small amounts, and if possible at the beginning of a meal.

As hunger is so important to eating it is wise to arrange conditions for stimulating hunger – sufficient time between meals and a regularity that conforms to the rhythm of the child. Eating between meals should not be too prevalent. Mid-morning fruit juice and biscuit for the toddler may be allowed if it is properly spaced between the breakfast and lunch hours. A glass of milk in mid-afternoon should not interfere with hunger if it is given at least two hours before the evening meal. Hunger is also helped by sufficient exercise and fresh air, but since fatigue hinders hunger it is necessary to guard against exercise to the point of exhaustion. It has been found helpful to have the very young child rest just before his meals. A ten-minute period when the child relaxes on the living-room rug before meals is a routine that pays dividends.

Emotional disturbances hinder both hunger and appetite. In fact, many of the eating problems of young children can be traced directly to emotional causes. When mealtime is unpleasant, the child's appetite suffers. Too much concern, too much urging, and the child reacts by refusing to eat at all or at least by eating very little. Eating problems are often produced by the parents' worry about whether the child is eating enough. This anxiety leads the parent to try to hurry the child or to get him to eat more than he may need or have appetite for. Careful studies have shown that the best attitude for the parent to adopt in the eating situation is one of unconcern or of calm expectation that the child will want to eat what he is given. When Mother places a new food before the young child and says, "Now, I hope you will like this," but indicates her doubt by her tone of voice, it is inevitable that the child will hesitate and refuse the food. On the other hand, when the parent indicates that the child is expected to eat the food and like it, the child usually does.

Mealtime should be a pleasant time. All the surroundings should be such as to make it an enjoyable, unhurried, and pleasant experience for the child. For the infant and toddler conversation should not be too distracting. In fact, it is better to allow him to give his whole attention to the business of eating. The four- or five-year-old can eat and carry on conversations at the same time. Attractive dishes, food that is well prepared and served in forms that do not increase the difficulty of eating, considerable variety in colour, consistency, and flavour all help to increase the enjoyment of eating and thus the appetite of the child.

As soon as the child shows any desire to do so he should be allowed to start feeding himself. He starts by holding the cup and spoon and by the time he is about two he does the whole job for himself. The young child is usually eager to do things for himself and any show of interest on his part indicates that he is ready. Of course, at first he will spill and make a mess, but this is an essential part of learning and is to be expected, not deplored. The transition from being fed to feeding himself should be gradual. At first, he merely helps to hold the cup or spoon; then he takes it himself for part of the meal, and, finally, he is doing it all.

It is advisable that the infant or pre-school child eat by himself rather than with the family. The family meal is too distracting, the child's food is probably different, and the whole situation is such that the process of learning good eating habits is hindered. Furthermore, some members of the family may have food dislikes, or food peculiarities, from which the child should be protected as long as possible. A high chair is undesirable since it is too much of a temptation to push it up to the family meal table. One of the best things to do with a high chair is to cut off its legs and make it into a low chair. At about the age of two the child can sit up at a small table. Since he will find it difficult to sit still for a whole meal, a kind of cafeteria system can be used, with the child bringing his plate for each serving and carrying it back to the table to eat it. In this way, his desire for activity is satisfied, but his meal is not too disturbed.

Servings should be small and the child allowed to have a number of helpings. In this way the child will get a more balanced meal; he will tend to eat some of everything, not finishing up what he likes best and leaving what he likes least. That dessert is served only when all of the first course has been eaten is a very good rule. It is just as well to have a time limit so that, if the child dawdles over his food, he finds that the meal is over and that he gets nothing more until the next meal. In this way he learns that mealtime is the time for eating not playing. We hope that he will learn a businesslike attitude to eating.

Table manners are not important for the pre-school child. He can and will learn them later. For the time being he should not be distracted, or have the situation made too difficult for him by insistence on manners. If he lives in a family where good manners are practised, he will almost automatically adopt what the rest of the family does.

Sometimes the young child uses mealtime to get attention. This almost always happens when there is too much parental concern about whether or not the child eats. When coaxing, pleading, or offering a reward for eating are used, the child soon learns that he can get almost anything he wants, including a lot of attention, from other people if he just holds out a bit. It is best to leave the child alone with the food, indicate that this is the time for eating, and have a time limit on the meal.

Forcing the child to eat or trying to force the food into the child is never a good idea. It makes the eating situation so unpleasant that appetite for food is destroyed. When the healthy child refuses to eat, it is a sign that there is something the matter. It may be that he is overtired, that some infection is present, that the meals are not properly spaced, that he has been eating between meals, that the process of elimination is not functioning properly. It is important to find out the reason for his lack of hunger and appetite rather than to force food into him.

By way of summary, here are some simple practical suggestions:

1 Make the mealtime a happy, enjoyable experience for the child. This aids appetite.
2 The infant and toddler should have his meal by himself away from the distractions of the family meal.
3 Give the child his meal in small helpings, allowing a second and third helping if desired.
4 Have the meals at regular hours. Except for mid-morning and mid-afternoon liquid and biscuits, allow no eating between meals. Candy, if allowed, should come after the meal.
5 Introduce new foods, new utensils, and new conditions one at a time. Introduce new foods at the beginning of the meal and in very small amounts.

6   As soon as the child shows interest, allow him to start learning to feed himself.

7   Each course should be finished before the child gets the next course. Have a time limit on the meal.

8   Do not coax, force, or in any way show concern about whether the child eats or not.

9   Introduce the child gradually to the family meal situation. Make it a privilege and a reason for learning to eat efficiently.

10 Do not emphasize the importance of eating. Do not tell the child that such a food is good for him.

11 Set a good example. Do not discuss food dislikes or food problems in the child's hearing. Help him to think of eating as a desirable, enjoyable, and natural activity.

12 If the child dawdles over his food, do not try to hurry him, but enforce the time limit. Show no concern, but assume that he does not want the food and make sure that he gets none until the next meal.

13 If the child shows a dislike for a food, allow no substitutes but require him to eat only a very small portion. Do not make an issue of it or allow it to become a cause for battle. If he chooses not to eat it, show no concern, but adhere to the rules of no substitute and no dessert until he has cleaned up his plate. Enforce the time limit.

14 Do not allow the child to succeed in using mealtime as a means to attract attention to himself. Do not make a game out of eating; keep it a businesslike activity.

15 Remember that there are great individual differences in the amount of food required. Healthy growth and vigour are better than any table of amounts as an indication that the child is eating enough.

Chapter 8

Character Education

IN A TIME of moral uncertainty and change there seems to be no question more pressing for parents than the development of moral values in their children.

Character development in children[1]

Philosophers (and others) have argued for centuries about the origin of character and ethics. Most parents want their children to be "good" and to grow up to be "good" men and women. Character is indeed a fundamental concern of parents. But what is good character and how does it develop?

Research has as yet provided only partial answers to these questions. Studies have thrown some light on how character develops but what constitutes good character is a matter of judgment and not something that can be answered by experiments. Good character is more than being good. The child can be good because he is afraid of the consequences of being bad or because he wants the approval of his parents or other rewards. On the other hand he can be good because he has accepted goodness as desirable in itself.

Children are not born good or bad. They do not become saints or criminals because of their heredity. Character is acquired. "You can't change human nature" may be truth or nonsense depending on what is meant by human nature. The individual is human in that he has the same basic needs and similar potentialities as all other human beings. He needs air, food, water, sleep, change, and activity. He has multiple potentialities for thinking, feeling, and learning. Each person is unique in the details of these potentialities. The kind of person he will become is determined to a greater extent by what happens to him after birth than by any of his inborn characteristics whether they be needs or potentialities. The experiences he has, the treatment he receives from parents and others, the opportunities he has for learning, the nature of his environment, and all the myriad influences that make up his own world will determine his character.

The young child is selfish or at least self-centred; his own satisfactions are all important. Naturally he seeks pleasure and avoids pain. It is only

1 K. S. Bernhardt, "Character development in children," *Bull. Inst. Child Stud.*, 1963, 25(2), 1–7.

after years of experience that he begins to move out of the narrow circle of personal satisfactions and to take into account the feelings, rights, and satisfactions of others. This progress is made partly because he slowly discovers that his own pleasure is somehow bound up in the pleasures of others. The infant is not yet ready to think of the pleasure and convenience of others; if he is hungry at 3 AM he cries, even though it means that his mother (or father) must leave a warm bed and needed sleep to satisfy his hunger. It will be some years before he learns to be considerate of others.

Ethics are basically concerned with the relationship of people to one another. One of the basic problems is to find a balance between self-gratification and interference with the self-gratification of others. Every child has to learn to achieve his satisfactions without coming into conflict with others or interfering with their search for the same thing.

A line of research started by Piaget in 1932 indicated that the development of moral judgment advanced in stages. The first level is that of obedience (guidance) of an individual. The good is what mother says is so, and her curbs, directions, punishments, and disapproval indicate what is bad and thus prohibited. The next level is that of rules and the child's guide to what is right is found in these rules. Rules later merge into principles and become less absolute. Circumstances are then taken into account, and intention, motivation, and values take precedence over absolute rules. The "spirit" of the rule becomes more important than its "letter."

The same developmental picture can be indicated in much the same way by describing kinds of conscience and their modification. The first and simplest conscience consists of a series of remembered "dont's," simple specific prohibitions. The second level of conscience consists of a desire to follow whatever the trusted and admired adults require. This conscience is really an expression of the child's attempt to win and hold the approval and acceptance of his parents, especially mother. The third level consists of an organized body of moral rules which serve as a guide for behaviour. This "living by the rules" may not require much understanding of the reason for the rules or of the varying circumstances which may even invalidate them. The highest level of conscience consists of internalized moral principles which are subject to rational questioning and testing. The content of these guiding principles includes values and attitudes which are both rational and emotional, that is, which include both understanding and acceptance and a strong desire to live by them.

There are three aspects of moral development, (1) intellectual – knowing what is right, (2) motivational – wanting to do what is right, and (3) behavioural – what is actually done. Knowing what is right and doing what is right do not go hand in hand. The child (or adult) can know that something is wrong and still do it. Knowledge is not enough, there must also be desire. Consequently the motivational aspect is the link between knowledge and behaviour.

This blending of the rational and the motivational elements of experience seems to be the key to character development. Good character depends on an understanding of the essential interdependence of people and a realization that consideration for others is an essential part of self-fulfilment.

A study by Peck and Havighurst (1960) provides much valuable material on character development. We shall not attempt to summarize this study here but shall select some conclusions and implications for mention.

Perhaps the most important of these conclusions is that by the age of ten in most cases, perhaps earlier, the character of the child is likely set for life. In this connection it is suggested that the only efficient way of ensuring good character is to work with parents before and soon after the child is born. This suggestion brings both hope and despair to those interested in character development – hope, in that good character is built in good homes, and despair in that deficient homes inevitably produce poor character. The endless chain of poor homes producing people who in turn produce poor homes can only be broken by an adequate programme of parent education. As the authors put it, "the general conclusion seems inescapable that a child's character is the direct product, almost a direct reproduction, of the way his parents treat him. As they are to him, so he is to all others." Of course, most of us have been sure that the example of parents is an important factor in character development, but this study goes even farther. It states that "to an almost startling degree, each child learns to feel and act, psychologically and morally as just the kind of person his father and mother have been in their relationship with him."

The Peck and Havighurst study and other related studies provide some details of this powerful character-forming influence in the parent-child relationship. The two basic parental functions are the provision of affection and the provision of adequate discipline. Both are essential, but obviously the nature of each is important. Parental affection can be shallow and selfish or blind and possessive, so that the child is treated like a pet or is trained to unthinking obedience. But parental affection which is warm and continuous and which accepts the child as a person in his own right and provides chances for him to develop his own individuality is an essential ingredient of good character development.

Lack of discipline or inconsistent control produce inadequate character development. Severe, autocratic discipline whether consistent or not leads to passive conformity and failure to advance to the final stage of moral development of understood, accepted, and functioning internalized principles. Consistent, reasonable, trustful discipline which provides practice in decision-making leads to self-disciplined persons. Mature parental love and rational, adequate discipline usually go together and when they do we have the necessary condition for both healthy and adequate character development.

Another approach to character formation in children through family influences can be found in a description of the factors which have been shown to be related to the desired result.

THE NATURE OF THE PARENT-CHILD RELATIONSHIP

This can be described by a number of dimensions such as acceptance–rejection, degrees and kind of affection, approval–disapproval, trust–lack of trust. There can be no doubt that good character stems from a relationship that shows a high degree of acceptance, an overall approval, a high degree of trust, and above all a warm affection that does not smother or overprotect the child.

In other words, the child who feels that he is wanted, accepted as a person, generally approved of, trusted and loved enjoys an atmosphere in which he can learn and develop and build a strong, healthy character.

THE NATURE OF CONTROL

While children are growing up there must be controls to protect them from danger, to keep them from interfering with others and from being destructive. These controls can also serve the purpose of helping the child to learn how to behave appropriately in a variety of situations. While controls are indispensable, the kind of control used is related to character development. All indications point to the superiority of democratic over authoritarian methods as the basis of character development. Democratic methods are based on such principles as: individual personality is more important than institutions; external control should be at a minimum; individual choice and decision are important and freedom and responsibility must go together.

THE PRINCIPLE OF CONSISTENCY

There is abundant evidence that consistency is an essential condition of adequate learning. A good scheme of discipline is only possible when the requirements and their enforcement are highly consistent. It has been shown that the home which provides the setting for desirable character development is one which is highly consistent in the treatment of the children.

SEVERITY OF PUNISHMENT

It is quite clear that severe punishment does not result in good character. There is a widespread idea that the simplest and surest way to produce goodness is to punish severely every evidence of badness. The truth is that severe punishment inhibits the development of good character. Punishment breeds resentment, desire for revenge, hostility, and other manifestations inimical to good character. The punitive approach with all its overtones of extreme disapproval, blame, pain, and fear is not conducive to the development of the understanding and the feelings of friendliness, trust, and affection which are necessary conditions for good character development. The child can be helped to learn how to behave by methods which are instructive rather than punitive. Very few, if any, children become delinquent because they have not been punished enough and many children are delinquent because they have been punished too frequently.

The home, then, is by far the most powerful agency for building character. In fact, there is no substitute for a secure home. Neither school nor social agency can supply the lack if the home is deficient. In the Peck and Havighurst study it was concluded that the steady, attractive example of wise and loving parents was the only influence which produced children with the highest level of what they called rational-altruistic morality.

Many parents are concerned about "bad companions" and the influence of the peer group on their children. It has become clear that these influences do not change in any important way the character formed in the home setting. The child's contacts with other children provide him with opportunities to try out what he has absorbed in the home. The basic trends in his behaviour resulting from the treatment he has received at home may be strengthened or reinforced by his experiences outside the home but not changed radically.

The same may be said of other influences such as movies, TV, and comic books. These will be interpreted in the light of values, attitudes, and motives developed in his relations with his parents. The community agencies for character education such as the Church, Scouts, Camps are no guarantee of good character since again they will function in the context of home influences. If the home has been adequate, then these agencies will support and reinforce, but if the home has been deficient it is unlikely that they will help very much. Parents cannot expect to hand over moral training to others, but parents who do their part can get help and support in their efforts from outside agencies.

It is clear that character development in children is not simple, not achieved by any simple formula or formal character education programme. Character is not a separate dimension of human nature, it is rather the quality of the total make-up of the individual. Good character is not just keeping out of trouble or living by a set of rules. Perhaps the most universally accepted (but not necessarily practiced) expression of good character is the Golden Rule.

There have been many descriptions given of good character and many attempts to identify its elements. A simple list of qualities of good character would include love, justice, and courage. The child develops love and justice by being loved and treated justly, and the child thus treated has the strength to develop moral courage.

Love is a much used and abused word. It means many things to many people. Here, we use it to mean an attitude towards people which includes unselfishness, consideration for others, co-operativeness, kindness, sympathy, loyalty, and altruism. Such an attitude transcends rules, codes, and standards, but finds expression in all social contacts and relationships. It is the quality that makes civilized living possible. The child who lives in an atmosphere of this kind of love slowly but surely absorbs it and his ability to love stems from his feeling of being loved.

Justice takes us beyond the narrow limits of relationships with those who love us and whom we love. It is, however, the expression of the same basic attitude. It is an extension of the idea of fairness and consideration for others to all people. When we feel warm affection for a person, we cannot be mean or unfair to him, rob or cheat him, hurt or bring pain to him. Justice is the extension of this same treatment to include those outside the circle of personal affection or liking.

Moral courage as a quality of good character is the ability to control any tendencies to let expediency or primitive selfish inclinations determine behaviour. It takes courage and strength of character to maintain the love and justice which are its hallmarks.

The following are some suggestions for adults interested in the character development of children:

1 Character education is inevitable and continuous. Every experience

leaves somes effect on the child. The cumulative result of these hour-by-hour experiences is character. Character education is not a separate, special programme, it is rather all that happens to the child in the process of growing up. Adults dealing with children always have a double responsibility. They must take care of the present situation, whatever it may be, but they must do so with a view to the developmental effects of their treatment. Not only do they have to consider how they can get the child to do something or keep him from doing something, but also what effect the experience will have on the developing personality and character of the child.

2 Character is most important in relationships with other people. One thing is abundantly clear in that the child acquires his attitudes towards other people from the attitudes shown towards himself by the important people in his life. He learns to love by being loved. He learns to be just be receiving just treatment. No amount of teaching or preaching can be a substitute for acceptance, affection, and consistently just treatment.

3 Character development takes time. The foundation of good character is laid in the first decade of the child's life. What happens in these years will determine to a large extent the character of the individual. During these years the child builds his knowledge of what is right and wrong, what is good and bad and what society requires. He also acquires his basic attitudes towards others, his values, and his guiding principles. All these things he absorbs from adults he admires.

4 It is very easy to fall into the temptation of thinking that the simple techniques of punishment aid character education. Severe punishment can produce outward conformity, but it fails to develop good character. Good character is not just the inhibition of impulses to undesirable behaviour. It is the development of a positive attitude which finds expression in rational, altruistic behaviour. The child who receives understanding, direction, and re-direction gradually builds up this attitude.

5 Preaching, exhorting, moralizing are a waste of time unless the behaviour of the adult conforms with the preaching and then the behaviour will speak for itself. On the other hand, explanation and discussion can be very helpful. The child has so much to learn about his world, especially the world of people, that he needs the help of understanding adults.

6 Historically, fear has been used to try to keep people good. Increased understanding of child development indicates that fear should be replaced by understanding. Good character has a rational base while unintelligent conformity is largely emotional.

7 There are no simple techniques of character education. The use of stories, ceremonies, ordeal, sports, and games may play a part but it is a minor one. For the child nothing can substitute for the experience of living in a home where he is wanted, accepted, and loved and where he receives consistent, just, and understanding handling by parents who respect him as an individual.

Character begins at home[2]

At birth the child is a bundle of potentialities; he can become almost any kind of person. His character, that quality of behaviour by which people label him as good or bad, will be the result of the experiences he has as he grows up. It is the product of his training in home, school, church, and community.

The development of sound character involves acquiring knowledge and understanding, building right attitudes and desires, and learning how to behave. Let us see what is involved in each of these.

KNOWLEDGE AND UNDERSTANDING

Good character depends on an understanding of the structure of society: a realization of what others do for us and how we depend on them; an understanding of the meaning and necessity of co-operation; and insight into our social responsibilities. It means also that the individual realizes the necessity for rules and restrictions; that belonging to a group (family, team, community) requires acceptance of these rules and limitations. Of course, these sound adult and require considerable experience to be in any way complete, but a start can be made in the early years. In fact, it would seem that if such a start is not made this kind of knowledge and wisdom is rarely acquired.

RIGHT ATTITUDES

Good character implies healthy attitudes, feelings, and motivation. These include the desire to be good and to fulfil obligations to others; faith in good causes; a determination to achieve the best of which one is capable. Good character requires the possession of a set of values and a

2 K. S. Bernhardt, "Character begins at home," *Bull. Inst. Child Stud.*, 1952, 14 (3), 1–4.

code of behaviour based upon them. These attitudes and motives require years to achieve, but foundations can be built in the early years.

DESIRABLE PATTERNS OF BEHAVIOUR

We usually judge a person's character by what he does, how he behaves. Some of the factors which we consider as indications of good character are: the direction of one's life with a minimum of supervision and control, habits of good workmanship and enjoyment of the effort, the habit of willing co-operation with others, the ability to get along with others both in work and play, by habitually displaying justice, fair play, honesty, truthfulness, sincerity, and dependability. A person of good character shows courtesy and good manners in his frequent services to others; he defends the right; he shows a generous spirit and protects the weak. Obviously a person embodying all these virtues at all times will rarely be found, but the start towards these desirable qualities must be made in the early years of childhood.

METHODS OF CHARACTER EDUCATION

Since character education is continuous and inevitable, all experiences contribute something to it. The general atmosphere of the home and school and other community organizations has more influence on the character of the child than any specific and deliberate educational method. However, some of the prevalent methods of developing character include the following.

Traditional discipline

Perhaps the most universally used method of character education is the application of traditional rewards and punishments. Goodness is rewarded and badness is punished, but it is hard to be consistent. Actually goodness should need no reward and badness should bring its own undesirable consequences without any artificial punishment. It is easy to bribe a child to be good but such bribery rarely helps to produce good character. This is also true of scaring the child to keep him from being bad.

Exhortation and preaching

Of all the common methods exhortation and preaching have the least effect; the adult's preaching often fails to correspond with the adult's behaviour. Children learn quite quickly to close their ears to frequent adult exhortation. Parental preaching is easy but most of it is a waste of time.

The story

Children's stories used to end with "the moral of this story is . . . ." We have learned to be a little more subtle and have tried to make the story yield the moral indirectly. For young children at least, the level of generalization and application required by this method is beyond their ability. Stories may be effective with adults but have little moral value for children.

Ceremony

Ceremony as a technique has held a prominent place in many character education agencies, the Boy Scouts for example. It can be an interesting, enjoyable part of such a programme but appears to have but little lasting effect on character.

Ordeal

The idea persists that character requires pain and ordeal, that character like gold is refined through fire. It is true that the child who has things too easy and never has to work hard tends to be soft and give up quickly, but the child's normal world provides plenty of challenge if too much protection is not afforded by misguided parents.

Sports and play

Many people think that if the child plays enough games and is on enough teams he will automatically learn fair play and sportsmanship and these qualities will in turn automatically carry over into other areas of activity. Unfortunately many children learn just the reverse of fair play in athletics today as they imitate the win-at-all-costs tactics of some professional athletes. Play and games, like many other activities, can afford a very good setting for character formation if attention is focused on co-operation rather than on competition and the child is allowed to gain satisfaction from participating.

Discussion

This can be a very valuable means of helping the child to form attitudes and acquire ideas and understanding. It is very difficult for most adults to take part in a discussion of life situations with children without "laying down the law" and being authoritative. This, of course, destroys the value of discussion. Free discussion, however, in which various points of view are expressed and the child both talks and listens can be helpful to him in increasing his understanding of social structures and meanings and in forming his own set of standards and ways of thinking and acting. The parent who refuses (or neglects) to listen to the child's comments about a movie he has seen, a book he has read, or a conversation he has heard loses an important opportunity to help the child to sort out his ideas and values. Informal discussion of everyday experiences is one of the most powerful character-forming methods we possess.

Counselling

Counselling may be defined as the intimate contact between two individuals in which one seeks to help the other in some way. The understanding adult, parent, or teacher can help to re-direct the child's thought and attitudes through such individual discussions. Although this method is used mainly when the child obviously needs guidance, it can be useful also when no particular problem is involved.

Practice

In one form the practice method is rather sterile. The child is required to do something a great number of times in the hope that a habit will be formed and as a consequence no further pressure will be required. This seems to be the reason for compulsory Sunday School attendance. Experience indicates, however, that when the pressure is removed the so-called habit disappears. Meaningful practice without external pressure is different and may best be considered as participation.

Participation

Participation provides meaningful experiences for children in which they can relate their behaviour to its results. They participate in life situations that are real, both in terms of the activity and its consequences. The adult's contribution is in "stage-setting," that is, in arranging the environment of the child so that he is exposed to such learning.

Social contacts

The most effective character education comes from contact with people who have good standards of behaviour and live by them. Most attitudes, manners, and morals are acquired by a process of absorption. The child who lives with people who have healthy social attitudes of tolerance and co-operation, thoughtfulness and consideration usually develops the same attitudes. Ideals are acquired by living in a social environment where such ideals are present and practiced. However, not all virtuous people are interesting and the child will expand his contacts beyond these paragons admired by his family. This need not alarm us; when the home foundation is solid, such associations will strengthen his character by teaching him an appreciation for and understanding of "all sorts and conditions of men."

Community influences

There can be no doubt that the nature of the community in which the child lives has a great deal to do with the kind of character he develops. The films he attends, the radio and TV programmes he hears and watches, the attitudes of the neighbours, the clubs or community groups he joins, the children he plays with, all contribute something to his character. It is clear, therefore, why it is important that parents work for community betterment.

Character is the product of the kind of training the child receives. Character education is not a separate department of education; all education is character education, and good child training in the home and school is the foundation upon which it is built.

Influences – good and bad[3]

We as parents in our awareness of the effect of experiences on the developing child have become concerned about the nature of these experiences. Every experience changes the individual to some degree. I suppose it is a realization of this fact that has caused so much concern about television, films, radio, comics, trashy literature, and a host of other modern influences which today surround the child.

Generally we parents have expressed our concern in a rather unfortunate way. We have said to ourselves that these things are not wholesome, they are not good, therefore we will shield our children from them, we will protect our children by banishing them from their lives. We have failed – and failure was inevitable for we forgot that the best way to make a thing more attractive is to put it out of bounds. Censorship

3 K. S. Bernhardt, "Influences – good and bad," *Parent Educ. Bull.*, 1942, no. 20, 2–5. Revised by D. K. Bernhardt, 1967.

usually defeats its own purpose. Tell a child that a particular book is not to be read and he can hardly help but accept the challenge – it must be interesting if the parent thinks it necessary to keep it out of his reach. That film is not for you – and the child wants to know why it is banned. I suppose we cannot help but be concerned about the intellectual and emotional diet of our children – what they hear and see and are exposed to – but this concern defeats its purpose when it takes the form of attempting to "protect" the child.

COMICS

Parents have been worried about comics for as long as there have been comic strips, and that must be for over fifty years. What are they worried about? They say that the child will pick up vulgarisms, that he will be overexcited by the adventures, that the humour is crude, that the children might get ideas for pranks and delinquencies. Parents are eager to have their children read only the best. They are anxious that the child should not miss "good literature" by spending his time reading "trash." I am reminded of the father who talked so often about "good literature" and the waste of time that occurred from reading what he called trash that his son took years to recover from his distaste for anything that could be labelled "good." I am reminded also of the young man who came to college and spent most of his first year reading the "trash" that his protective parents had deprived him of while he was at home.

There is one fact that we must not overlook, that children need to identify themselves with their contemporaries. They must know what their companions know, must be able to talk and listen in the language of their group. We cannot neglect the fact that television and comic strip characters are almost national characters – part of our folk lore – and the child (and even adult, for that matter) who does not know them is to a certain extent "out in the cold." There is room for what we call good books and bad comics, but there should not be a ready-made classification into good and bad. The child can be guided, but he should not be forced to accept any such classification. The development of his power of discrimination is the most important thing, and to discriminate he must know.

The problem then, it seems to me, is not how to exclude the comics and related literature, but how to bring into the picture other kinds of reading as well. I think that the most effective way is to let interest do its work. The parent who is interested in a wide variety of reading matter, who does not obviously try to force his interests on the child, who is ready to talk about what he reads and listen to what the child has to tell about what *he* reads can have a lasting influence.

Part of the appeal of the comic strip or comic book to the child is the way it is put together. It makes liberal use of pictures, it deals with life situations, it has dramatic suspense. But the comics have no copyright on these factors. Books for children are much more attractive than they used to be. You can lead a child to books, but you can't make him read what you think he should, at least not by direct methods. However, he will read what he is interested in and what is available. Books and magazines should be made available and under no circumstances should the child be presented with anything in the nature of a challenge – to read this and not to read that. Censorship is out.

MOVIES

Some of the things I have said about comics also apply to the movies. When all the children in the neighbourhood go to the movies on Saturday afternoon, it seems hardly fair or desirable that your child should not do "what is done." Of course, intelligent parents want their children to enjoy the best and to see only the good pictures. This may be not only impossible but even undesirable. It sometimes happens that those children who are exposed only to the "best" revert to the crude and the vulgar. The way to develop taste and discrimination is not to forbid and censor but to guide the child to an understanding and appreciation which can form the basis of wise and discriminating choice.

Sometimes boys and girls rebel against the too insistent requirements of their parents that they should only see the best – when the best is interpreted in terms of the adult's standards. There are so many situations in which parents have to insist, to require, to prohibit that it would seem as though the movies could be left to the child when he becomes ten years old. That doesn't mean that there should not be some kind of guidance, because guidance is necessary, but the guidance need not be out and out prohibition.

The movies are an important part of our current life, they are not all bad by any means. Going to the movies is what is done by the group, and talking about the movies is a daily activity. Of course movies as a steady diet, as a regular pastime can easily push out many other more beneficial activities. It isn't so much that movies are a bad influence, or that the child gets a distorted view of life, for these things can be corrected, but that the movies can crowd out other things that may be of more value to the developing child. The movie is a spectator not a participator experience, and as such has or should have only a limited place in the life of the active child. But movies *do have* a place. They offer a world of entertainment as well as of education and can lead to valuable discussions both with other children and with parents. The parent who says in a tone of disgust, "Don't talk about that trash in this house," when the child starts telling about a movie he has seen, is doing much more harm to the child than any movie can, no matter how bad it may be.

There is very little that parents individually can do about the kind of movies produced, except to patronize those that are good and refuse to attend those that are cheap and undesirable. However, groups working together can and should make their voices heard, not just to condemn but also to praise those that deserve it. In movies as in most commodities, we get more or less what we want and are prepared to pay for. Children take their lead from us. They learn to discriminate by having frequent opportunities to experience, to choose, and to discuss.

TELEVISION

To many parents television is enemy number one. In many families it causes more discussion than any other single situation. Parents complain about the low standards, the exciting and even terrifying programmes for young viewers; they complain that television makes bedtime enforcement difficult, that it interferes with homework, and that children watch it instead of being out of doors or playing at more creative activities.

Children will watch television and they will watch the programme that everyone else is watching, but like the movies television is not all bad, and like the movies it is an important part of modern life. In other words, children like to keep in the swim, to know what is going on, to be able to talk about those programmes that other children talk about. Here is another situation that calls not for censorship but some rather skilful guidance.

What does the child get from television? What wants is he trying to satisfy? I suppose the most important thing children are seeking is excitement. Why? Perhaps because their lives are so regulated, so uneventful, so ordinary. They are looking for adventure, and in most cases they are finding it vicariously. With very few exceptions it does them no harm. They seem to be able to keep this vicarious adventure in perspective. It isn't real, but it is fun. It doesn't seem to matter to the young viewer that the hero is left in the most dangerous situations until the next instalment. He knows that the hero will be saved, or the programme couldn't go on. There is the occasional child who is so upset and excited by this kind of programme that he can't sleep. This child should be protected from such programmes or at least he should have his watching restricted to small doses. The majority of children, however, can stand the excitement.

RADIO

Many of the comments made above can be applied to radio, although in most homes the television set is now much more of a problem. One of the worst present-day habits is that of having the radio on but not listening directly to it. This practice is understandable; if the radio is not on we might miss something. But the picture of father reading his paper, the children doing their homework, mother writing letters, with the radio blaring in the same room, seems to be somehow distorted. It is an indication of a failure to choose and it poses a dangerous challenge to concentration.

Like reading, the movies, and television, radio provides a passive, spectator rather than participator experience. As we mentioned before, there is a place for such experience but a rather small one. When being a spectator becomes more enjoyable than doing, making, and being active, when passive listening becomes an escape from all participation, then we should become concerned enough to do something about it.

The only effective way to ensure that the movies, television, radio, comics and other such spectator activities do not occupy too large a place in the child's life is to provide opportunities, ideas, and materials for other kinds of activities. If at least half the energy we now use in trying to combat what we consider undesirable influences were used in devising ways and means of finding equally interesting substitutes for them, we would be much further ahead. The child should be encouraged to develop ability in activity requiring the use of his hands. It may be playing a musical instrument, using tools, painting, making things out of clay or wood, sewing, knitting, cooking, or any one of a host of other truly participator activities. It could be collecting, nature study, or sports. In fact, there are innumerable activities and experiences possible if the child gets a little leadership, guidance, and example.

I have discussed comics, movies, television, and radio, which, of course, represent only a few of the influences in the world of the child. There are many more: the community in which he lives, the church and Sunday School, the gang, organized groups such as Scouts and Cubs, his school, and his home. I don't think it is possible to divide these influences in the life of the child into two categories – good and bad. No one of them is all good or all bad. Their influence depends on how they fit into the total picture; whether there is a balance between being entertained and participating; and on whether the child is helped to assimilate his experiences and gets practice in discrimination.

No matter how powerful other influences are, no matter how important the contribution of the school, the church and the community is, the quality of the home is still the fundamental influence in the life of the child. It is the home that either fails to help the child to evaluate and understand what he experiences or is successful in giving a tone, an emphasis, and a meaning to the various experiences. The home is still and must remain the basic educational institution in the land.

REFERENCES

J. Piaget, *The Moral Judgment of the Child* (New York: The Free Press, 1965) (original edition, 1932).
R. F. Peck and R. J. Havighurst, *The Psychology of Character Development* (New York: Wiley, 1960).

Chapter 9

Education for Family Life

THIS CHAPTER[1] not only examines the question of sex education (a far more controversial topic when Karl Bernhardt dealt with it than it is today) but also looks at the questions of training for responsibility, learning to manage money, and training in work habits.

TWO FAMILIES

Nearly everyone knows two families well – the one he grew up in and the one he helps to establish. The education received in the first will help to determine the management of the second. It is becoming increasingly clear that the factors which govern success or failure in marriage and family life have their beginnings in the early years. The individual's best guarantee of success in marriage is a happy, healthy childhood and adolescence in which he has met successfully the problems of adjustment. The attitudes, patterns of behaviour, goals, and values which the young adult brings with him to marriage are the product of his previous experience, the kind of treatment he received in his first family, and the opportunities he had for learning.

The success of individuals in marriage is not as high as we could hope for or expect. The increasing divorce rate, the frequency of desertion, separation, and marriage breakdown provide abundant evidence that there is plenty of room for improvement in education for family life. We are confident that more and better preparation for marriage would reduce the failure substantially. The most important aspects of this preparation take place in the individual's first family. If his life in this first family has provided him with adequate knowledge, healthy attitudes, and a sufficient degree of social and emotional maturity, he should have a reasonable chance of achieving a happy and effective marriage adjustment. In the following sections we shall describe some of the essentials of an adequate preparation.

SEX EDUCATION

That sex is an important part of life is accepted by nearly everyone. We live in a sex-saturated society. Sex is exploited by advertisers, fiction writers, film producers, TV programmes, and by individuals who seek attention or publicity. A child whose sex education is derived from the stories and conversations he hears, the programmes he hears and sees, the newspaper accounts of sex deviates and criminals, the cheap fiction of the pulp magazines cannot escape having a distorted and unhealthy picture. Yet one of the essentials of a successful marriage is a healthy attitude to and adequate accurate knowledge of sex.

1 K. S. Bernhardt, "Education for family life," *Bull. Inst. Child Stud.*, 1962, 24(4).

Sex education should be a family matter. In reading childhood histories written by university students I have been amazed at the frequency of the comment, "My parents gave me no sex education at all." These are young people from good homes, not in the Victorian age but in the world of today. Most parents readily agree that sex education is important, but many do not know how to impart it, and many freely admit that they tend to shy away from the subject with their children.

Some parents are willing and even eager to surrender to the school, church, or community agency the responsibility for sex education. It is true that parents should expect some help from these organizations, but it is also true that the home has the primary responsibility, simply because the important first steps in sex education take place in the years before the child starts to school or participates in community activities. Furthermore, the child builds his picture of the meaning of marriage and family life mainly from what happens in his own home.

In considering sex education, it is easy to make the mistake of thinking of an "occasion" or of a set of "facts of life" to be given to the child at some appropriate time. Adequate sex education, however, is a long, gradual process, made up of hundreds of incidents, experiences, and comments. Facts are not enough. Children need more than information. Attitudes, point of view, means, and emotional colouring are even more important.

It is a mistake to think of sex education as no different from any other topic. A topic so interwoven with the intimate personal life of the adult cannot be in the same category as arithmetic or spelling. It is not surprising that many parents find sex education embarrassing or even impossible to handle. For such parents a programme of self-re-education is in order. The development of a more objective and relatively impersonal attitude is possible by reading, study, thought, and discussion. One small group of mothers solved this problem by meeting together a number of times and taking turns answering such questions as young children ask. In this way they managed to reduce their embarrassment and became more familiar with the words used in talking about the body and its functions.

OBJECTIVES OF SEX EDUCATION

In any plan of education, a set of clear-cut objectives is essential, since it is only when we know what we hope to accomplish that adequate planning is possible. The following suggestions will serve as a starting point in the defining of objectives. Each parent, of course, can build his own goals; the following suggestions are offered merely as a guide.

1   Provide information for the child when he asks for it or is ready for it. The information should be adequate, accurate, adapted to his level of understanding and satisfy his present curiosities.

2   The development in the child of attitudes towards sex which are healthy and objective, and which do not burden him with apprehension and worry.

3   The gradual building of acceptance of sex as an important but natural aspect of living with anticipation of the responsibilities and joys of marriage and family life.

4   The development of an understanding and acceptance of the sensible and necessary social conventions related to sex.

5   The building up and maintaining of confidence and trust in the parents so that the child will always feel that he has a source of honest information and a place to discuss his fears and worries when they occur.

ACCURATE INFORMATION IS IMPORTANT

The simple answer to the question, "What should we tell the child?" is "what the child wants to know." The young child is curious about everything he sees and hears. He wants to know what makes the sun shine, where the rain comes from, why it gets dark, and where babies come from. And he should know. His natural honest curiosity deserves frank, honest answers. Of course, a three-year-old child cannot understand the whole complicated story of human reproduction, but he can understand a simple account of the growth of the baby in mother's body and how he is born when he is big enough and strong enough. He can understand and appreciate the fact that father has some part in it and that babies must have both fathers and mothers. He can understand that girls are different from boys and in what ways, and, to a certain extent, why – that girls grow into women and mothers, and boys into men and fathers. It is easy to make the mistake of trying to tell too much all at once. Usually the young child's curiosity is satisfied with a simple item of information, and we count on many occasions to gradually build a complete and adequate picture. Simple questions call for simple answers. Later, when the child is older, he may ask much the same questions, but now the answers can be more complete. If the channels of communication are kept open the child will continue to seek information from his parents. If he does not, we should take pains to see that confidence is restored.

There is no sure guide as to what information is needed by the child at any stage of his development. In general it can be said that simple foundations are laid in the pre-school years when the child asks questions about where babies come from and about sex differences. In the school-age period the child's fund of information can be gradually increased as opportunities arise. Before puberty the boy and girl should have a fairly complete knowledge of the changes that will occur in both the growth of the body and the biological urges which accompany them. The girl should be prepared for the dramatic happenings at puberty so that she will understand the meaning of woman's monthly cycle and realize, for instance, that menstruation is not a sickness but a normal function. The boy, also, needs preparation for puberty so that he too will understand the meaning of the changes he is experiencing.

An adequate account of human reproduction is essential knowledge for the young adolescent. Books and pamphlets help but should not be thought of as a complete substitute for discussion. The adolescent should be helped to think of reproduction as a family function, that mating and marriage go together as do sex and love. Above all, the attitudes and feelings about sex need to be healthy and not furtive and secretive. There are so many indications in the world of the adolescent that sex is nasty, dirty, and sinful that counteracting influences which say very clearly that sex in the context of the family is normal and even beautiful are needed.

For the school-age child difficult questions and problems can arise from news reports and conversation. Topics such as sex deviates, prostitution, and unmarried mothers fall into this category. Often a very brief explanation that avoids giving them an emphasis that is out of proportion to their importance will suffice. Sometimes the normal and desirable is brought into focus by the deviations, which can be discussed as unfortunate forms of sickness or behaviour arising from ignorance or distortion. Open, frank discussion rather than avoidance of topics is the most important thing.

In adolescence, such practices as dating, petting, going steady call for attention. The most important single factor here is an obvious trust by the parents of the adolescent. This show of confidence accomplishes much more than moralizing, preaching, or forbidding in helping the adolescent to build his own standards of behaviour. The parent need not hesitate to express his point of view and his standards of behaviour, at the same time indicating his firm belief in the adolescent's ability to manage his own affairs. This kind of confidence can be built only on a foundation of both adequate information and healthy attitudes.

Parents of young adolescents and the adolescents too could read with profit the book written by Evelyn Duvall, *Facts of Life and Love for Teen-Agers*, which is available in a paper-book edition.

Although correct and adequate information is of central importance, it is not by any means the whole story of education for family life. There is no sure formula for making certain that young people will manage their sex lives happily, but when they are brought up in happy families and have guidance that is both sympathetic and understanding their chance of achieving a happy, successful marriage is good.

TRAINING IN RESPONSIBILITY

Education for family life includes training in responsibility. This, like sex education, is effective when it is a gradual and continuous process from infancy to maturity. By responsibility we mean the acceptance and the fulfilment of the obligations of social life without reminder or direction. The responsible person is reliable and dependable. Successful family life is impossible without responsible adults.

The child learns responsibility by practice, that is, he is given a little at a time, with the amount gradually increasing as the months and years pass. The child is put "on his own" for some aspects of his daily activity. He is given the responsibility for the management of some of his time, personal care, and possessions. It can start with small things and gradually expand until, by the time he is an adolescent, he manages nearly everything for himself.

This training requires that the parent be ready to "let go," to allow the child to grow up. It means that the child learns by accepting the consequences of his failures. He gets no practice in responsibility as long as he is treated as a mere child who must be regulated even in the smallest matters. Many a boy or girl has left home with very little practice in managing his own affairs, possessions, money, or time. Is it any wonder that some of them find in difficult to manage the complex affairs of a new home?

LEARNING TO MANAGE MONEY

There are many aspects of the kind of maturity essential for successful marriage and family life. One very good illustration is the management of money. There can be no doubt of the importance of money in family life. Although failure to manage the family finances adequately may not cause family breakdown, it does make happy efficient family life difficult, if not impossible. Practice in the handling of money helps prepare the individual for family living.

Such practice can and should begin early in life. The child should have a regular, limited income to manage. Managing means spending, giving, and saving. Later he can have the experience of earning as well. Starting with a small weekly allowance, the amount at first covers the modest needs of the young child which he can look after himself. The income gradually increases as he learns to plan and manage for himself and the areas covered by the allowance expand. By the time the child has reached his teens, he can control most of the money the family can provide or he can earn to look after his personal needs, including clothes, carfare, school supplies, and recreation.

A very important part of this training is participation in the financial affairs of the family. He can learn about banking, budgets, insurance, mortgages, pensions, investments, and related matters. He can take part in family planning and discussions and in this way gain knowledge and experience in the complex business of managing family finances. This, too, can start in a small way, but by the time he leaves home to help found another, his knowledge in this area will be adequate.

TRAINING IN WORK HABITS

The mark of a well-functioning family is the participation of all its members in the work of the household. Certainly a man who cannot change a fuse or hang a curtain rod or a woman to whom a cook book is a closed book are hardly educated for family life.

From an early age the child can have a hand in the work of the family. He can be helped to feel that he is a contributing member of the group doing his share of the necessary work. He is not merely "mother's little helper"; the work he does is *his* share of the household tasks. He can be helped to acquire skills and competence as well as interest in and even enjoyment of some tasks. Boys should not learn to think of some household work as being exclusively feminine, nor should girls be excluded from practice with paint brush or screwdriver.

Perhaps the most important feature of this training is in the fostering of attitudes towards housework. The child who thinks of housework as a burden or even a necessary evil is not well prepared for the founding of a new family. It is true that appliances and gadgets have reduced household tasks considerably. It is also true that the community provides many services which used to be part of the work in the home. But work still remains to be done and the willing acceptance of one's share of this work is a part of the maturity required for success in marriage and family life.

It is often easier for parents to do things themselves than to try to get the children to participate. However, the extra planning and effort in involving the children are desirable. Once a week the family can discuss the work to be done and divide it up, with each member having some choice in the tasks for which he will be responsible. This procedure should help to establish the idea of the group approach and the meaning of group membership. It also helps to provide some variety and avoid monotony and dislike for some of the work. It makes very clear to each child that belonging means doing one's share.

REFERENCES ON SEX EDUCATION

In addition to the many books on sex education, an excellent variety of films, filmstrips, and records is also available.

For young children: Gruenberg, S. M. *The Wonderful Story of How You Were Born* (New York: Doubleday, 1952).

For pre-adolescents: Johnson, Eric W. *Love and Sex in Plain Language* (Philadelphia: Lippincott, 1965).

For adolescents: Duvall, Evelyn M. *Love and the Facts of Life* (New York: Association Press, 1967).

For parents: Child Study Association of America. *What to Tell Your Child About Sex* (New York: Permabooks, 1958).

Chapter 10

Feelings and Emotions

Children's emotions can be respectable[1]

Most of us behave as though emotions were hardly respectable. Yet emotions are as much a part of human nature as breathing or thinking. What is more, emotions can be a very valuable part of an individual's approach to the problems of everyday living.

For a long time now society has considered emotion to be a sign of weakness and has exerted pressure on people to hide it. Hence, without realizing very clearly what they are doing, most parents try to train their children to stifle their emotions. For example, tears are thought of as childish, something to be outgrown as soon as possible. "Don't cry" is an almost universal parental entreaty. In many ways a young child is reminded that he should not be angry or afraid. Even though he cannot *help* being angry at times, it is made clear to him that he should neither show his anger nor feel it. Naturally, all children are sometimes afraid, but, if they show fear, adults usually voice their disapproval and other children call them sissies. It is essential for adults to gain a more understanding and sympathetic approach to the inevitable and natural emotional behaviour of their children.

THE SIGNIFICANCE OF EMOTIONS

Emotions are not separate and isolated from life; they are a part of the usual flow of experience. An emotion is a "moved" condition, an enhancing of activity, a sign of an emergency in the experience of an individual. Human nature is so constituted that when a person experiences either a threat to his safety or well-being or a hindrance to his wants his whole organism starts preparing for action. Such action may be in the form of attack or defence, or it may be to do something such as run away, in order to remove the threat or hindrance. Thus, emotions are related to problems, and problems are the everyday experience of every individual.

The intelligent, mature, and civilized way of dealing with problems is to find some way of overcoming them: to solve the problem; to avoid the danger; to find a way around the obstacle. This is the key to emotional education. Therefore, instead of training children to hide and deny their emotions, adults should help them to find ways of *coping with*

1 K. S. Bernhardt, "Children's emotions can be respectable," *Bull. Inst. Child Stud.*, 1959, 21(3), 8 – 12.

fear – or anger-producing situations. We can picture emotion as a dynamo of energy which needs harnessing and directing. The development of such control will take time, of course, and though a child may make progress towards it while he is young, his parents must not expect perfection.

FEAR AND ANXIETY

All children have fears, but great variations are observed in the number and intensity of those fears. Some children exhibit temporary fears which disappear as they learn more about their world and develop ways of coping with situations. Some fears, however, persist for years or even for life. Usually these are the fears which as children they have been led to hide or deny.

Many conditions have been shown to be related to the occurrence and seriousness of fears. One of these is the nature of a child's relationship with his parents. Fortunate is the young child who has parents who are both affectionate and consistent. This child can feel that he is accepted and wanted and at the same time know what he can expect and what is required of him. He develops a feeling of trust which is centred at first on his parents but which later expands into trust in himself and in other people. A child with this kind of healthy dependent security is not as susceptible to fears and anxieties.

Unfamiliarity, strangeness, or newness can produce fear. So much in the life of a young child falls into this category that it is surprising that his fears are not greater. The fact that a young child usually has someone who serves as a protector, a haven to which he can retreat, serves as a compensating factor. This someone is normally his mother. However, if his mother, in her zeal to have him grow up, fails to provide reassurance and a feeling of security, the child's fear can persist and grow into a general insecurity. Note that, along with reassurance and protection, there needs to be gentle guidance towards learning to cope with situations, and hence towards self-assurance. As a child learns to face and deal with new and strange situations, he gradually acquires the ability to face others and needs less and less the reassuring presence and support of an adult.

Other conditions which can cause fear in a child are being alone or being threatened with abandonment or loss of his loved ones. This type of fear and anxiety can take many forms, one of which is fear of losing the love and approval of his parents. Some children even have to face the cruel, thoughtless threat by their parents of being sent away. A child has no defence against this kind of threat and no child should ever be exposed to it. All young children need to be given the assurance that their parents will return, even though they may be away for a time. Happy is that child who feels that he can depend upon consistent, understanding parents.

A serious but also a rather common condition leading to susceptibility to fear and anxiety in children is exposure to belittling, ridicule, or disparagement. A child who is made to feel incompetent or inferior finds many situations frightening and productive of anxiety. His confidence in himself gradually diminishes and, finding situations ever threatening, he tends more and more to withdraw. What is worse, he becomes afraid of being thought more incompetent and tries to hide his fear. A really vicious circle is now established. A base of self-confidence is essential for children in order that they may meet and cope with the many new and strange situations with which life confronts them.

Another factor that increases the frequency and seriousness of a child's fears is the example given to him by the adults in his world. Fears and anxiety in his parents not only suggest dangers and threatening situations to the child but also tend to weaken the feeling of security and protection which he should have. More serious than this, the presence of fears in his parents hinders the normal development of the child's ability to face and cope with potentially fearful situations. One could speculate on the effect of the present world situation with its threat of terrible destruction on children. Perhaps parents would do well to spend less time listening to world news and talking about potential enemies and a third world war, if not for their own peace of mind at least for their children's sense of security.

Fear can be healthy and valuable when it leads to knowledge of how to deal with threats and dangers, but fears and anxieties that are not channelled into *adjusting activities* can be both disruptive and unhealthy.

A number of simple but important suggestions can be given for the prevention and conquest of fears in children. *Knowledge* sometimes banishes fear, especially when the fear is based on *ignorance*, but the knowledge which we provide for a child should be definite and specific as well as accurate. Vague general statements, such as "There is nothing to be afraid of," do more harm than good. As mentioned above, *example* is a great help. Perhaps the most effective method is to *help a child to deal directly with the feared situation*. The final goal must be reached gradually with the support and reassurance of the adult, for a child needs time to acquire skill and competence in dealing with both materials and people. Finally, *adequate preparation* for new experiences can be very helpful provided that the experience is not endowed with an importance that might intensify rather than prevent the fear. Forewarnings should be casual and not too emphatic.

ANGER, HOSTILITY, AND JEALOUSY

In general, anger results from hindrance or frustration of some kind. Hindrances may arise from a child's own ineptitude with materials that are difficult to manage or with his social environment. Necessary rules and restrictions can be hindrances. Delay in satisfying a need such as hunger can also act as a frustration. Some hindrances can be overcome by learning and acquiring skills, but some must be accepted as realities that cannot be removed. Training in adjustment to potentially anger-provoking situations takes two forms: (1) teaching a child how to solve the problems presented by hindrances, and (2) teaching him to tolerate and accept the necessary frustrations of living.

Anger is expressed by children in a variety of ways. In young children the expression is usually violent and intense, but of relatively short duration. As a child grows older he learns to direct his anger into language or more direct attacks; he also learns to reduce the violence of his outbursts. In healthy development the mobilized energy is directed into solving the problem presented by the frustration.

There are a number of conditions which increase a young child's susceptibility to anger explosions. A reduced level of energy is one of them. A tired child, a child who does not get enough sleep, a hungry child are examples. A child who, through his own ineptitude, is unable to do what he wants is frustrated and becomes angry. Even a reasonable scheme of discipline presents frustrating situations to a child. A child's inability to make his wants known makes him feel hindered and obstructed. Parents who overestimate the ability of the child can be disturbing, as can nagging or over-anxious parents. Any condition which puts a strain on a child is potentially anger-arousing.

Hostility is a more permanent emotional condition in which a child's smouldering anger is directed towards some person or persons. Sometimes the hostility is displaced and the child takes his anger out on someone other than a parent or teacher. Hostility is sometimes generated when the general plan of discipline is unreasonable or inconsistent. A child who has discovered that his explosions of anger succeed in getting him what he wants tends to continue to use this method.

Jealousy is a complex emotional condition in which both fear and anger are components. Jealousy is an indication that the child feels insecure in some relationship; he may fear that he is losing the affection of one or both parents. Along with the fear he experiences anger at the apparent cause of his loss. Jealousy frequently arises where there are comparisons between children or unfair treatment or indications of favouritism. A jealous child needs to be made to feel secure in the affection of his parents and this sense of security usually requires more than verbal assurance. The child should be treated as an individual and given adequate individual attention. Comparisons and unfair competition should be eliminated.

Emotions are respectable. They are an important part of a child's make-up. They can be used as the source of energy to tackle problems and acquire skills. Emotions bottled up, hidden, denied, or considered shameful can be dangerous. Emotions frankly faced and dealt with can be healthy. Parents who can accept the fact that children have emotions and that they express them in their own childish way, and who try to help their children to deal with emotion-producing situations, can help greatly in their development. Perhaps this – the understanding and effective handling of emotion in children – is the most difficult test of parenthood.

Feeling, affection, and happiness in children[2]

What is the most puzzling, interesting, and unpredictable aspect of human activity? Without a doubt it is what we usually call "feelings and emotions."

It is the feeling part of experience which not only makes life interesting but also directs much of what we do. Sentiments, moods, and the emotional dimension of human experience provide the colour, variety, and sparkle that rescue human experience from the dead level of routine and monotony. We may pride ourselves on being rational beings, but actually we are emotional beings. This is even more true of children than of adults.

Traditionally, childhood is a happy, carefree time, but observations

2 K. S. Bernhardt, "Feeling, affection and happiness in children," *Bull. Inst. Child Stud.*, 1961, 23(2), 1 – 5.

of children seem to tell a different story. A child's day is a mixed bag of happiness and unhappiness, joy and sorrow, satisfaction and disappointment, likes and dislikes, exciting activity and boredom; in fact, he seems to run the whole gamut of human feeling and emotions nearly every day. The young child is relatively uninhibited in his emotional expression, and his emotional experiences are relatively brief and alarmingly soon forgotten. No child is happy all the time and some children are unhappy most of the time. Children differ greatly in their customary or characteristic feeling pictures. However, everyone would accept that it is desirable, indeed important, that the child be happy most of the time, that his happy times outweigh his unhappy times.

This immediately raises such matters as frustrations, requirements, restrictions, punishments. It opens up the question: how permissive should adults be in dealing with children? And it seems to suggest that any restraint, compulsion, or pressure on the child should be avoided. But it is not as simple as this, because requirements, rules, directions and even restrictions are not necessarily unpleasant, nor do they lead to unhappiness. On the contrary, the child needs to know what his limits are and what is expected or required of him. He feels secure when he has a consistent but reasonable foundation in such knowledge.

What the child needs most for a predominantly happy feeling are: (1) a reasonably prompt satisfaction of his basic needs and (2) a thoroughly dependable relationship with his most important adults, especially his parents. He can meet most of his disappointments, failures, and frustrations if he feels that he is thoroughly accepted, loved, and understood by his parents, especially by his mother.

Children thrive in an atmosphere of affection that is intelligent and consistent. It is a source of difficulty that affection is sometimes taken to mean indulgence, inconsistency, and over-protection. It is sometimes interpreted as a way of controlling and directing the child. Children return affection when it is freely given and uncontaminated by considerations of control and restriction. One might say that the child must have people to love; otherwise he fails to learn how to direct his affections outside himself.

The normal development of the affections requires first a person, usually a mother, who is dependable and consistent and who provides a constant emotional haven. She is a protector, provider, and source of affection that never fails. In other words, this is the solid, reliable object of dependency in the child's experience. This is the foundation on which he can build his strivings and learnings – the harbour from which he can launch out to explore, discover, and learn, and to which he can return when things get too much for him. He has someone he can trust, on whom he can depend, and towards whom he can direct his feelings of affection. Without such an object for his affections, he has no foundation on which to build his developing social and altruistic feelings.

The undoubtedly serious damage to personality and emotional development reported in children who have suffered what has been called maternal deprivation is the result of this lack of trust and dependency and affection. Because the child has no one to trust, no ever-available person on whom he can depend, and no constant flow of affection, he feels insecure and his insecurity is such that he has no way of dealing with it. He can feel insecure and still learn when he has an adequate dependency relationship, but without this kind of relationship he is insecure in a more permanent sense.

Children thrive on affection and seem to be seeking it. When they feel the warmth of affection in another person, they respond in kind. Children learn to love by being loved, and it is in an atmosphere of affection that a reasonable scheme of discipline works best. The affection is the background for the discipline, not a part of it. In fact, affection should never become a part of discipline as such. When affection is used to control the child, it not only cheapens affection but it misleads the child into thinking that he should behave in certain ways either to earn, or to avoid losing, the affection of the parent. The time when the child most needs the feeling of being loved is when he is in difficulty.

At first the child's affection seems to be an extension of his feeling of pleasure and well-being, associated with the satisfaction of his needs. Later he extends his feeling of warmth and affection beyond the narrow boundaries of biological self-satisfaction. However, this development of positive, outgoing feelings for others must have the foundation of biological satisfaction on which to build. This is one reason why the infant should have the kind of care which yields a feeling of comfort and well-being. As he grows older, he needs the feeling of thorough acceptance.

Feeling is an important dimension of experience at all ages, but especially in early childhood. In infancy the meaning of an experience is almost entirely a feeling since there is very little past experience to provide meaning. Thus, the infant's evaluation of any situation is based almost exclusively on how he feels. Thus some situations mean to him satisfaction, pleasure, and contentment, others mean distress, discomfort, or even pain. This is the main reason why it is important that the infant be made as comfortable as possible and that his needs be satisfied promptly and adequately.

Gradually, as the child grows older and his knowledge and fund of experience accumulate, other aspects of experience play a more prominent part in determining meaning. Now he can begin to understand that he may have to wait for some satisfactions and that he cannot have everything he desires. Now he can accept these delays and frustrations because he is able to understand their reasonableness and necessity. However, even if understanding has increased, feeling is still prominent and important. No matter how rational he becomes he will continue to use feeling as an important element in judgment, choice, and the direction of behaviour as long as he lives.

Every experience, activity, situation, object or person will be given a feeling evaluation as either "pleasant" or "unpleasant," and such evaluations will vary in degree from extremely pleasant to mildly pleasant or unpleasant. The point I am making is that the way we feel about things helps to determine how we behave. This is the basis of what are usually called attitudes. An attitude is a tendency to behave in a certain way towards something. Thus we have attitudes of acceptance or avoidance towards people, activities, situations, or objects. One child likes school, teacher, and arithmetic. He puts effort into his school activities, getting fun and satisfaction in return, and his attitude is strengthened. Another child dislikes school or teacher or arithmetic or all three, and thus his attitude is one of withdrawal and avoidance. His effort is slight and his return in fun and satisfaction is almost non-existent.

The point of all this is simple but basic and important. How the child feels about things will have a great deal to do with how he behaves. Notice the difference between the child's activity in a self-chosen play situation and in some imposed task which he does not like. In the first, his enthusiasm and involvement are almost boundless, but in the second his reluctance and attitude of avoidance show that he is giving as little of himself and of his effort as possible. We are faced with something of a puzzle here, for it is impossible to have the child like all the activities in which he must engage. The answer is twofold: first, we make required activities as attractive and pleasant as possible, so that the child develops a positive attitude towards *most* of them; secondly, we help the child to accept the remainder as necessary and desirable, and to do them as quickly and as well as possible, so that he can get on with the things he likes doing.

This may sound as though we are suggesting that the child must never experience frustration, hindrance, or disappointment. Rather, we are suggesting that the child can handle such experiences better if the prevailing atmosphere is one that provides feelings of pleasure and satisfaction. The negative kinds of control seem to be easier, more available, and even necessary, with the result that the parent or teacher may find that most of his contacts with the child are of the negative kind – restricting, punishing, prohibiting, belittling, or condemning. The predominating feeling is then one of unpleasantness. When this happens, the child develops attitudes of withdrawal, dislike, and aversion. In other words, negative discipline creates negative feelings. All of this adds up to the necessity of seeing that the positive aspects – pleasantness, satisfactions, affection, acceptance, and approval – outweigh the negative ones.

Childhood should be a happy time, not only for sentimental reasons but because this provides the best foundation for healthy growth and development. Making children happy does not mean giving them everything they seem to want, pampering their every whim, and protecting them from all that is frustrating or unpleasant. Some of the child's happiness should spring from putting forth effort to solve his problems, learning to do things for himself, and overcoming difficulties.

There are always the two contrasting dimensions of feeling, affection, and emotion. Thus we have pleasantness and unpleasantness, comfort and distress, love and hate, like and dislike, and many similar contrasts. For the sake of clarity these may be considered as positive and negative. Evidence points to some simple conclusions. Life is always a mixture of the positive and the negative. When the positive far overbalances the negative, we have the necessary condition for the development of the child in a healthy and desirable way. The child's character and personality are the products of what happens to him, and the most important and powerful part of this is feeling.

Man has been asking for centuries what determines character and personality. Research workers have been trying to unravel the tangled skein and find definite answers. It will be a long time yet before we have most of the detailed answers, but we can be sure that feelings and emotions play a large part in character and personality. We can be equally sure that the developmental trends of feelings and emotions started in early childhood will continue and will exert a powerful influence on the personality structure of the individual. These developmental trends are the result of the atmosphere in which the child grows up.

Chapter 11

Leisure Time

KARL BERNHARDT explores in this chapter the many activities available for the leisure time of the child. Both solitary activities and activities for the family and the peer group are discussed. Today more than ever before it is important for the child to learn at an early age how best to use his leisure time. Closely related to this topic is the article in chapter eight entitled "Influences – good and bad."

Summer is a time for play[1]

School's out! To some parents this means the bother and nuisance of looking after the children all day. To others it means family fun. Parents are pretty evenly divided between the two groups – those to whom the children are a worry and a nuisance and those who enjoy the children. It's a fundamental difference and a rather searching test of parenthood.

Few people today still hold the old-fashioned idea that play and fun are evil, but there are many who think of them as frills and luxuries. There are still others who have no time for play – life is so serious and full of important work that play and fun get crowded out. No matter how busy we are, there must be time for play, because play is indispensable. The person who can't play is the person who is inevitably inefficient at work. Play is needed for relaxation and recreation and to satisfy the need for change and variety. Without play Jack (and Jill too) will be not only dull but unhappy and inefficient as well.

Leisure is time in which we are free to do whatever we like. Leisure is not idleness. It is activity devoid of the element of compulsion. Leisure activities are those which are chosen because we enjoy doing them, because we want to do them, and because they satisfy the deepest needs of our personalities. In such play activities we get release from the tensions and strains of living. This is true for all ages.

SUMMER ACTIVITIES FOR THE CHILDREN

Given half a chance, children both enjoy and profit from play. "Half a chance" implies time, place, materials, companions, and ideas. There's nothing quite as tragic as the bored child, whether he be two or fifteen. The bored child is the unhappy child and the unhappy child is a nuisance and a liability. The parents' responsibility is to provide time,

1 K. S. Bernhardt, "Summer is a time for play," *Parent Educ. Bull.*, 1946, no. 36, 3–7.

place, materials, companions, and ideas, as already mentioned. The parents do not need to regiment, restrict, control, and manage the child's play life, but children *do* need direction, and this direction is best given unobtrusively. The parents' job is that of stage manager – shifting scenes and properties to provide a new challenge and new ideas.

For the infant under two, play is rather simple – a few basic playthings, a play pen in the shade, and an absence of adults. This is the time when "leave him alone to play" is the fundamental rule. Of course, the play materials should be safe and the adults not far away, but the infant should not need to be entertained.

For the pre-school child the picture changes in detail but not in fundamentals. Again it's a matter of providing the setting and leaving him alone to work out his own play pattern. If you have managed the stage-setting successfully, he will be able to amuse himself in a constructive way. He will show interest and the beginnings of concentration. If you have failed, he will be bored, destructive, unhappy, or dependent on you.

The pre-school child still needs to be protected from the consequences of his ignorance. This means enclosed play spaces, safe materials, and supervision. Supervision, although necessary, should not be managing supervision or stimulating direction but a kind of "nearby in-case-of-need" function. Too much assistance, direction, and stimulation of the young child hinders his development towards independence and makes him look more and more to adults for help and direction.

The pre-school child needs companions of his own age some of the time. He also needs time for solitary play. The summer provides opportunities for co-operative supervision by parents of pre-school children. Whether in the city or at the summer cottage, usually there are other pre-school children not too far away. If the parents can get together, select one backyard or play space, equip it with suitable materials, set a block of time each day, and take turns supervising the group, both the children and the parents will have a happier and more profitable summer. Of course, this play group should not be an all-day affair; about two hours each morning will suffice.

There is often a tendency to get away from a regular routine in the summer. This may be acceptable for older children and adults, but the pre-school child needs the solid security of regularity and consistency. There will be fewer difficulties if the pre-school child has his meals at regular hours, a regular afternoon sleep, a regular time for play with other children, a time to play alone, and a time to take part in family fun.

A word about materials – for it is the materials that provide the ideas and create interest, and it is materials, not elaborate toys, that the pre-school child needs. Sand, water, clay, mud, plasticine are always play materials for the child. Blocks, paper boxes, cans, indeed almost any objects which we throw away can become parts of the summer play pattern. Dolls, wagons, kiddie-kars, trucks have their place. The important thing is that the child have something to use. It is a pathetic but too frequent sight to see a young child "put out to play" with nothing to play with. And don't forget the rainy days and the need for indoor play materials – books to look at, old magazines to cut up, small blocks to build with, plasticine, crayons, paint, coloured paper, scissors, and housekeeping toys.

THE SCHOOL-AGE CHILD AND HIS SUMMER HOLIDAYS

There are plenty of things for the school-age child to do, but some careful planning is necessary. This planning includes an arrangement of time so that there is a place for the home chores which are an essential part of his day but also time for uninterrupted activities. It also includes providing the materials and opportunities for interesting activities.

If the school-age child spends his summer at a cottage, the activities are usually "ready-made" – swimming, boating, building, riding bicycles, sports, and games. If he spends his summer in the city or town, more planning is necessary and trips, excursions, picnics, both with the family and with his friends, have their place.

Here is a list of some leisure-time activities for school-age children. Remember that there should be a balance between spectator and participator, active and passive, and solitary and social activities.

1 Sports, games, and athletics
2 Group games, indoor games, and games of skill
3 Handicrafts, building and construction
4 Collecting (almost anything)
5 Art – sketching, painting, modelling, carving, etc.
6 Photography
7 Music – producing and listening
8 Dancing
9 Reading
10 Dramatics
11 Cooking, especially on the campfire
12 Gardening
13 Exploring nature and the world
14 Keeping pets
15 Camping
16 Hiking

These activities are discussed more fully in the next article. Remember that your child is growing up and that more freedom and a wider range both of territory and activities is called for.

IF YOUR CHILD GOES TO CAMP

Summer camps will be full and many children will be unable to attend because there will be no room for them. The summer camp is an institution that is becoming more and more accepted as an important part of our Canadian life. The camp can and should become even more important, for the camp can provide a kind of experience that is unique. Practice in intimate group living, lessons in co-operation and tolerance, first-hand experience with nature, chances to learn self-reliance and independence, and opportunities for creative expression are only a few of the many values in the camp experience for children. The scope of the camp will be widened. Now it is mainly for boys and girls from about 8 to 16. There is a place for adult camps, for family camps and for co-educational camps for adolescents.

Here are some tests that can be applied to camp, which at present fall into the categories of good camps, poor camps, and camps that only partly live up to adequate standards.

1 *Safety* Are there adequate safety precautions in regard to swimming and boating, riding, and shooting? What about the sanitary precautions? Is the water properly tested? Are the kitchen and the kitchen help clean? Are there adequate provisions to prevent and care for possible illness and accident?

2 *Supervision* Who are the staff? What is their background? Have they the necessary training and knowledge for their jobs? Are there enough staff members for the number of children in camp?

3 *Program* Is the program well planned? Does it take into account the fact of individual differences? Is it rigid, does every child have to do the same thing at the same rate at the same time or is it flexible, providing opportunity for a great variety of activities without undue regimentation? Is there plenty of chance for self-chosen and self-directed activities?

4 *Routines* Is there a well-established, planned routine in which the child gets regular meals, regular sleep, and rest? Does the camp aid in developing hygienic habits of living?

5 *Social* Does the camp provide opportunities for development through satisfying practice of the qualities of a good citizen? Is there provision for the development of initiative, co-operation, leadership, followership, tolerance? Are courteous consideration of others and the obligations of social life a part of everyday living?

6 *Sports* Does the camper develop a variety of sports in which he can

participate with increasing skill and satisfaction? Are some of these sports ones which he can carry on in later life?

7 *Aesthetic* Does the camp provide opportunities to experience and appreciate the beautiful? Is there a spirit of reverence for the good, the true, and the beautiful? Is there guidance for the camper and is there a good example?

8 *Attitude* Is the camp a happy place? Is there wholesome comradeship, free from sentimentality? Is there in everything the joy of living? Is there adventure and the spirit of discovery? Is there friendship and faith in the goodness of human beings? Is there a feeling of freedom and responsibility? Is the general atmosphere happy, healthy, and wholesome?

These are tests that might equally well be applied to a home, or a school, or a community. The answers to these questions determine pretty much whether the environment is rich in those factors that make for healthy growth and development, or whether it hinders and stunts such growth.

FAMILY PLAY

When the family plays together its bonds are strengthened. Summer can be fun for all the family if we do a little planning. This planning can ensure that there are plenty of chances for the family to do things together. When the children share their experiences with father and mother, the parents can get better acquainted with their own children and appreciate them more, and the children can discover what fine people they have for parents.

There are literally hundreds of family activities – some work, some play. We shall mention only a few, letting the reader think of others. There is, of course, the family picnic, which takes many forms. Its essential value is that all members take part in the planning and preparations. Then there is the exploration of one's own community – the parks, beaches, zoo, museum, art gallery, and other features which visitors see but residents usually miss. Each member of the family can have his turn in choosing the family excursion.

The family project – garden or basement, any kind of construction – with all members taking part should be mentioned. This type of activity has almost limitless possibilities. And, of course, there are any number of games both for indoors and outdoors in which all the family can participate.

In work as in play the family can share experiences and have fun. The members can take turns planning and preparing meals. The home chores can be divided up or shared. Mother can have a holiday too if all members of the family take a hand in the work of the household.

The main thing is that the family should play together and have the fun of doing things together. It will be strengthened as a unit, and the individual members will be healthier and happier and better prepared for another year of living.

Leisure time activities for the school-age child[2]

No one today doubts the importance of leisure-time activities in the lives of school-age children. Some of the most important character and personality features are developed through leisure activities. Initiative, resourcefulness, intelligent planning, persistence, and the fine art of enjoyment are just a few of the traits developed in this way. Every child needs time that is all his own to do with as he pleases. No amount of planning for him, of scheduling music and dancing lessons, of clubs and classes, scouts and guides can be a substitute for exercising his own choice and carrying out his own ideas.

There is no lack of entertainment in the modern world. In fact, there is probably an overemphasis on being entertained. There is a place, of course, for listening and watching but doing and making and creating should not be crowded out. Many children spend endless hours at any kind of movie. This is their sole idea of an afternoon's entertainment. These "passive" pursuits have an important place but not, as we have said, if they crowd out more active leisure-time activities.

1 *Games* Sports and athletic games are many and have become well known through their use in schools, camps, and recreational organizations. It is important that they should not be too complicated for the child and that competition should not be overstressed. There are also many games, such as cards, checkers, croquinole and other table games,

2 K. S. Bernhardt, "Leisure time activities for the school age child," *Bull. Inst. Child Stud.*, 1951, no. 49, 3–6.

puzzles, games of skill in which several members of the family can take part, which can help to keep the home happy. Besides pure enjoyment and the skills developed, these provide opportunities for learning both how to win and how to lose gracefully. This in itself is quite important.

2 *Handicrafts, building and construction* There is nothing quite as satisfying as making things, and there is an almost unlimited variety of materials and kinds of products which can be constructed. Wood, leather, metals, plastics, clay, paper, yarn, cloth, linoleum can provide some of the materials for construction. The products are limited only by the materials, tools, time, and ideas available. A place to keep the materials and tools, a place to use them, and some help and encouragement are all needed.

3 *Artistic and dramatic activities, art, music, dancing* All these activities offer a variety of interest. Art includes sketching, painting, modelling, and carving. Given the materials, the child should be free to experiment and create his own productions. Music can be for some children an absorbing and enjoyable activity for leisure time, provided their acquaintance with it is not limited to adult-imposed music lessons. Phonograph records, family orchestras, occasional concerts, and the judicial use of radio are all aids to musical appreciation and production. Dancing, if not spoiled for the child by too much formalization, can be a happy form of expression as well as an aid to co-ordination and poise. Dramatics may be enjoyed through watching a play or participating in it. There are a number of ways in which the school-age child can satisfy his desire to be an actor – marionettes and puppets, as well as the staging of an original play by young authors and actors. Dramatic play is prominent in the play of young children and it carries on for some time. Dressing up, using make-up, putting on a circus, a play, or any kind of performance can be a happy occasion in the life of the child.

4 *Exploring nature and the world* Each is an endless source of joy and interest. In exploring nature a child discovers there are many wonderful things that happen out-of-doors. He doesn't have to go to the zoo or out into the country to see them happening – wind, snow, rain, sunsets, frost, insects, birds, plants, flowers, all these and many more can be found in the backyard. Then there is "astronomy." This may interfere with bedtime occasionally, but the values and fun the child may receive from the study should be ample compensation. A small telescope, charts of the heavens, and simple books on astronomy are all that the child needs who is fortunate enough to have a parent or friend who can share this interest with him.

It is a particular nature interest for the child to have pets and to care for them. The variety of pets is almost endless: kittens, dogs, canaries, white rats or mice, guinea pigs, rabbits, fish, turtles, to name a few. For the city child trips to the farm to see the domestic animals and to get to know them can be both a joy and an education. Another form of exploration is that of the world around us. This can take the form of visits to nearby points of interest as well as longer trips. Above all, the child should learn the joys of seeing. Factories, stores, fire-halls, museums, art galleries, the station, the post office, are just a few of the places where children can see and learn, and in so doing gain an appreciation of the kind of world in which they are living.

5 *Home arts* Cooking – both boys and girls may have fun producing culinary masterpieces, and the rest of the family can enjoy the results. Like all leisure-time activities, materials, opportunities, and a little guidance must be provided along with a feeling of freedom – something for the child to do because he enjoys it. Gardening – there are many exciting moments in caring for growing things. If this is to be a truly leisure-time activity it too must convey the feeling of freedom – it's the child's own garden, and he cares for it because he wants to.

6 *Collections* Building up a collection of anything – stamps, coins, match-box folders and classifying, mounting, and caring for it offers many joys and advantages.

7 *Reading* This occupation opens up great new worlds to the child. The greatest danger is that reading may become too engrossing and push aside more active forms of enjoyment. Although the child needs some guidance, he should not feel that the adult is selecting his reading or imposing standards on him. He should develop his own standards of criticism. A lot of what he reads adults may call "trash," but some of this trash is a help in many ways. That the child should learn to discriminate is the important thing, not that he should learn to accept what others say is "good literature."

8 *Listening* The radio, the concert, the movies, the play, and even the lecture, all have their place in leisure activities even if they are passive, spectator pursuits. But they provide only one way, and not the major way, for the child to spend his time.

PRINCIPLES OF PLANNING FOR LEISURE

1 *Time* It is necessary to plan the child's day so that there is time for him to follow his own interests, time that is as uninterrupted as possible, and time that the child can feel is his own. There should be no desire or

attempt on the part of the parent to make every moment count. In these busy days it is necessary to guard children against that constant pressure of time that is so characteristic of modern living.

2 *Materials* Most leisure activities require equipment, tools, raw materials of some kind, this adults find one of the most difficult features of leisure time activities to handle. They complain that the child does not use the materials they provide, that his interests do not last, or that materials are too expensive. Two very good principles to follow are: (a) provide materials in terms of the child's expressed interests, but start with the simplest and gradually increase the amount and kind of equipment as his interest continues and grows; (b) provide materials to stimulate, never to force, interests, and always keep the age and ability of the child in mind.

3 *A Place* For most leisure activities the child needs a place to keep his materials, tools, and collections, as well as a place to use them. Every home has places that can be fixed up with shelves and cupboards. These are indispensable for the child. Of course there should be reasonable requirements about putting materials away and clearing up, but continual stress on tidiness takes all the joy out of the activity.

4 *Attitudes* The attitudes of the parents and other adults have a great deal to do with the development of interests in the child. Interest breeds interest. There are many activities of the school-age child which do not seem worthwhile from an adult point of view but which are very valuable to the child. The adult should respect the child's choice of activity and remember that there are individual differences in what people enjoy doing. One of the easiest ways to stifle interests is to try to impose or force our adult interests on the child. He needs plenty of encouragement and help, but this should take the form of stimulating him to choose and initiate activities for himself.

5 *Example* The adult who has his own interests and obviously enjoys his leisure provides an example which is most effective in producing the same kind of behaviour in the child. Remember the busy child doesn't usually get into mischief.

SOME GENERAL PRINCIPLES ABOUT
LEISURE-TIME ACTIVITIES

1 Permanence of interest in some particular activity is not to be expected and is not desirable. The school-age child changes his interests fairly frequently. Although this is disturbing to the adult it is probably beneficial to the child because he thus explores the realm of leisure

activities and acquires knowledge and skills which can be the foundation of his adult interests and hobbies. He should be encouraged, however, to continue his interests long enough to judge whether he has exhausted the possibilities of the activity for the time being.

2   A variety of interests is desirable. Too much specialization is to be avoided during this period. Activities which are both individual and social, spectator and participant, passive and active are necessary.

3   The emphasis should be on the enjoyment of the activity more than on the achievement. Thus awards, competition, display are minimized and the fun of doing the thing for its own sake is stressed rather than the product or the result.

4   The child's leisure should be both in and out of the family. Family leisure activities – the sharing of activities by all members of the family, doing things together, with parents and children on a level of equality – have a high value. The family functions as a more effective unit when there are plenty of family excursions, games, music, art and craft activities in which all members of the family take part. On the other hand, there should be a recognition of the importance to the child of having interests and activities beyond the family circle.

Present-day life can be so strenuous and serious that play has become even more important. Let us help the child to play and let us not forget to play ourselves.

Reading for pleasure[3]

It is amazing how few adolescents read books for pleasure. I haven't any reliable statistics to quote, but in interviewing adolescents I have found a large number who read books only because their teachers require it. Most of them find it a burden, not a pleasure. I can't help but think that there must have been something wrong with their introduction to books. A visit to the public library would convince anyone of the potential pleasure packed between the covers of the thousands of good books for boys and girls. Any boy or girl introduced to this treasure-house of adventure, beauty, and knowledge would surely form a lifelong habit of reading for pleasure.

Some children develop an abiding love of books. These children are

3   K. S. Bernhardt, "Reading for pleasure," *Bull. Inst. Child Stud.*, 1952, 14(4), 9–12.

introduced to books early; their parents usually love books, and long before the children have learned to read, they experience the joy of owning and using picture books and of hearing stories read to them. All children like stories, and when they realize that most stories come from books, they are ready, as soon as they can read for themselves, to explore the wealth of fiction that books will provide. All children are curious about the world in which they live, and thus it is easy for them to discover that books will tell them much that they want to know.

Some parents succumb to the temptation to exhort their children to read "good" literature and not "trash." The difficulty is that the children enjoy what the adults label trash, and so such exhortations succeed in making the "good" literature forbidding. It seems important for the child to sample a variety of books so that he can gradually develop his own standards of taste and preference. He may concentrate on the comic book for a time, but if other types of literature are readily available he will try them too, and the chances are that he will discover much to interest him and give him pleasure. Reading "good" books should not be a duty or a burden but a joy. Perhaps the greatest influence in this regard is an atmosphere in which books of all kinds are accepted as a pleasant part of living.

While no other reason is needed for helping the child to acquire a love of reading than the pure joy and pleasure he will receive, there are other values which might be mentioned. Books help to develop the imagination and widen the horizons of the child beyond the seen and the heard. Books are a storehouse of knowledge and the child can learn much about the world and people from his reading. Reading can become a healthy form of relaxation, a way of using part of his leisure time, a habit which can be continued throughout his life. Living can never become dull and commonplace for the individual who can explore new realms of human experience through the pages of books. Reading stimulates intellectual growth and provides material for thought; it provides the material for the building of ideals, ambitions, and attitudes. Reading should make schoolwork more interesting and richer in content. These are some of the many reasons why it is worth the time and effort of parents to help their children develop habits of reading for pleasure.

CHOOSING BOOKS FOR CHILDREN

Although there are some books with an almost universal appeal, it is nevertheless more true of books than of movies that the tastes and interests of children differ enormously. It is unfortunate that most children's books are selected not by the child but by his aunts and grand-mothers. Yet they can select wisely if they try to remember that the book is not for themselves but for Charlie or Margaret, and consider what Charlie is like and what Margaret is interested in or could be interested in.

In choosing a book for children there are a number of things to be considered: we should ask (1) is it well written? is the language clear, and the ideas well expressed; is the structure such that it provides a good model for imitation? (2) Is it suitable for the child's level of mental development? (3) Is it likely to fit in with the child's present interests or develop those interests? (4) Is it wholesome and worthwhile in content? (5) Is it well printed, bound, well illustrated, durable? (6) Is it something you want to have the child treasure, read, and re-read? (7) Is it something the child himself wants?

The child's age has an important bearing on his reading interests. There are great individual differences but in general four-, five-, and six-year-olds like illustrated stories about familiar things: home, animals, nature, rhymes, and simple poems. In the early grades boys prefer books about real people and animals and girls about other children, home, and school. Both boys and girls, however, enjoy fairy tales at this age. By about twelve, boys are looking for stories of action, excitement, adventure and sports, and inventions; girls are beginning to favour romance. In the early teens boys like hero stories, mystery, biography, history, and travel; girls tend more to romantic fiction. By sixteen their tastes are more individual, more specialized, and more adult.

A desire for the new and scorn for the old should not be allowed to keep each generation of children from discovering the treasures in some of the "classics." It was a very wise bookseller who remarked gently in reply to his customer's comment, "These are old books," "Yes, madam, but the children are always new." Some parents have the exciting experience of seeing their children discover books which they had loved. If, however, they expect that this will always happen, they are sure to be disappointed. Some of the books we loved when we were young may produce nothing but scorn from our children. As a boy I worked my way through a stack of Horatio Alger tales, but my son was bored with them and didn't finish even one of that once popular collection.

Children should own some books – books they can treasure and read over and over again. They need a bookcase where they can keep them and get at them whenever they like. But young people need not be limited to books they own, since every public library caters to the young reader. The great variety available, plus the understanding guidance of the librarian in directing the child's interest to this wealth of literature, helps to carry him far beyond the volumes he himself could ever own. The libraries through their trained children's librarians can also assist the child in the choice of books for his own collection. Leaflets such as Fifty Books No Child Should Miss, Good Books to Read, Pictures and Stories to Read, Tell and Show to Little Children can be sent for or carried home from many public libraries. A more extensive guide is available in the paperback edition of *A Parent's Guide to Children's Reading*, by Nancy Larrick (Pocket Books, 1958).

FAMILY READING

In spite of radio and television, movies, and commercial recreation, some families have managed to retain that greatly rewarding experience of sharing their reading. Family reading takes many forms: sometimes reading aloud, sometimes discussing books read by all, and sometimes describing what was discovered in books. It is a fortunate child who lives in a home where books yield pleasure and the enjoyment is shared. A charming account of the experience of one family with books is *Bequest of Wings* by Annis Duff (Macmillan, 1944).

THE CHILD WHO READS TOO MUCH

Some parents worry when their children "always have their noses in books." Some children become so interested in books that other things get crowded out for the time being, but with most children it is usually only "for the time being" and other activities soon take their place again. It is nearly always a healthy sign – it means that the world of books has become an exhilarating one to explore. Generally, the best advice is to let it run its course and hope that when the reading binge is over there will be a continuing interest in the treasures of literature. Once in a while we meet a child who has learned to escape from the world of reality, responsibility, and problems into the pleasant universe of books. Here we tread quietly and do what we can to re-direct him to everyday matters by making this world of reality more pleasant and still not spoiling his pleasure in reading.

Reading for pleasure can be a great aid to personality development if it takes its place as one of the activities of the child and later of the adult. Such activity makes life interesting to the individual and the individual interesting to others. He has an activity which can provide many hours of enjoyment, which enables him to entertain himself, and which has many valuable by-products. Happy is the child who has discovered the treasure there is in books.

Chapter 12

Mental Health

ONE OF THE AIMS of all the articles in this book is the development of positive mental health in the developing child, and one important factor in this development is mentally healthy parents. In this final chapter, Karl Bernhardt focuses on the development of positive mental health and offers a number of suggestions for achieving it.

Psychology of everyday life[1]

We have learned to manage nearly everything in our world but people. Our progress in learning to manage the physical features of our environment has been stupendous, but we seem to have failed to make a corresponding advance in our methods of managing human affairs. Our failures in human relations have outnumbered our successes. Witness the recurring wars, industrial unrest and strife, the frequency of family breakdown, juvenile delinquency, adult crime, and mental disease. In fact, human history portrays a succession of failures to manage human relationships effectively. And this has been true on the personal level as well as in terms of broader group activities.

This failure has not been entirely the result of ignorance, at least some of the knowledge required for effective social relationships is available. The failure has come partly from our neglect to use the knowledge that is available. For instance, although we know some of the more important factors related to marital adjustment, failure in this area seems to be increasing because this knowledge is not put into use. We know some of the causes of mental breakdown and yet our knowledge is not being applied adequately to stem the tide of unhappiness and distress from mental disease. We know how to prevent juvenile delinquency and yet boys and girls are still living in the kind of environment which produces such behaviour.

Mental health is a valuable personal possession. Many people lose it either wholly or in part; in fact, the mental health of all of us could be improved. Our mental hospitals are full, and although there are as many beds in mental hospitals as in general hospitals they still do not fill the need. A large percentage of the patients are sent home cured or at least well enough to carry on. Most of the cases of mental illness could, however, have been prevented, for most of them have no organic basis.

1 K. S. Bernhardt, "Psychology of everyday life," *Proceedings, Life Insurance Inst. of Can.*, 1947, 85–9.

In order to prevent mental illness and even more important in order to strengthen the mental health of all of us, I offer the following suggestions – suggestions in the form of everyday habits of thought, feeling, and action. If an individual possesses these simple but fundamental habits, his chances of maintaining a desirable level of mental health are good. They are so simple and so ordinary that many people will not take them seriously. They are not new or startling, they are common sense. More than that, they have a solid foundation in psychological knowledge. Here they are:

1 The habit of living in the present. The healthy individual focuses his attention mainly on the present. The individual who lives mainly in the past or in the future is not as healthy as he should be. True, the healthy individual profits from the mistakes and successes of the past and plans intelligently for the future, but his main focus of interest and attention is on the task or pleasure of the moment. He lives each experience to the full but only once. He does not waste his energy in living each experience three times – once in dread and apprehension, once in the experience itself, and once more in the "might-have-been."

2 The habit of living easily. This does not mean that the individual does not work hard, for hard work never hurt anybody. It means that he has learned to minimize the strains and stresses of everyday life; he has learned to take things as they come without too much emotional disturbance; he has learned to reserve his emotional disturbance for really important things. He does not let his whole day be spoiled by trivialities; he has a sense of perspective – has sorted things out so that he knows what is worth expending his energies on.

3 Healthy social contacts. The mentally healthy individual is adjusted to his social environment. He is not a "lone wolf." He enjoys the companionship of others. He is interested in people and in sharing experiences with them. Very frequently the individual who is not in good mental health is the person who has withdrawn from social contact, who is distrustful of other people, who has developed hate and suspicion of others.

4 The habit of making decisions promptly. This is a valuable habit because when the individual postpones a decision that must be made he places himself in a state of tension and conflict. I do not mean to suggest that the individual should decide things by the toss of a coin or make snap judgments, but I do mean that it is important to make a necessary decision as soon as possible. The principle is the same whether

the decision to be made is trivial such as what to have for dinner or more important such as a change of job or buying a house or choosing a wife. The important thing is to acquire the habit of making decisions promptly so that there are not too many uncertainties hanging over one's head.

5 The habit of keeping in touch with reality. This means facing the facts of one's own behaviour and avoiding too much rationalization. It means avoiding the extreme kind of day-dreaming in which the individual escapes from reality into a world of his own construction. It means the cultivation of an objective attitude.

6 The management of emotions. Many people are tortured by vague fears and feelings of insecurity which they will hardly admit to themselves but which keep them from many happy experiences and which tend to undermine their mental health. Fears are common to all human beings, but the dangerous fears are those bottled up within the person. It is wise to bring them out into the open for examination. Many people allow irritations, annoyances, and danger to dominate their lives. Most of these irritations are unnecessary and are about things which are forgotten even before the individual has "cooled off." But the aftereffects of the emotion are to be seen in lowered mental health.

7 The habit of cheerfulness and optimism. This is a valuable asset both in terms of social acceptance and in terms of personal mental health and happiness. I do not mean an unrealistic optimism, but I do mean a fundamental attitude that life is good and worth living. It is so easy to get into the attitude adopted by many of going around in almost continuous gloom and pessimism. These individuals can hardly be happy or healthy.

8 Sufficient interests. The mentally healthy individual finds lots of interesting things to do and no time to feel sorry for himself or ponder on his unhappy lot. He has hobbies, things he'd sooner do than eat. He is a participator not just a spectator. Life has zest for him. People who have never learned to play or find fun in work are usually neurotic or at least basically unhappy. Interests should not be too narrow but should provide changes of activity and scene for the individual.

9 The experimental attitude. Ruts are often so comfortable that the individual goes on in the same old way whether or not it is pleasant or profitable to do so. The healthy individual has learned to adopt an open-minded attitude and in his thinking, feeling, and behaving he is alive to a number of possibilities. He keeps himself from becoming too "set in his ways."

10 A sense of humour. This is essential to healthy living. I do not mean

the kind of humour that enables us to laugh at other people's mistakes and misfortunes, but the kind that enables us to look in the mirror and then laugh.

These ten suggestions for personal mental health can be followed by anyone. The outstanding feature of human nature, the ability to learn, is not restricted by age. As long as the individual is alive he is capable of learning.

Now to look at the problem of effective social relations. I shall offer a number of practical suggestions here too. Getting along with other people is an art that can be acquired. It depends on a number of basic attitudes and habits. Our failures in social relations are the result of the way we have been educated at home and school. We have been trained to think that the most important thing in life is to get ahead of others and to fear that other people will get ahead of us. We have learned also to be concerned about our own rights and to be on the lookout lest other people violate in some way these personal rights. In order to get along happily and efficiently with others these two tendencies must be modified.

Briefly, then, let me describe a number of simple principles for ensuring happy effective social relations:

1 Be genuinely interested in other people as individuals. Such an interest is not difficult because people are the most interesting things in our world. This means treating people as persons rather than as a means to an end, a mere number on a list, or just another customer.

2 Use sincere appreciation. An examination of almost any social relationship situation will reveal that words of praise, approval, and appreciation are usually few and far between, but there is nothing to surpass them in making for smooth, happy relations between people.

3 Eliminate as much as possible the use of criticism and disapproval, for these have just the opposite effect from appreciation. People become irritated and annoyed when they are criticized and belittled.

4 Let the other person discover and correct his own errors. Pointing out errors openly causes him to try to justify himself and to cover up his mistakes, thus hindering his learning.

5 Don't try to make over the other person openly. He will resent it and your relationship with him will deteriorate as a result.

6 Cultivate the habit of sympathy – the ability of putting oneself in

the other person's position and taking into account how he feels and thinks about things.

7 Cultivate the habit of tolerance. This involves the elimination of prejudging people on the basis of their race, class, or nationality. It means looking for the worth of the individual in spite of the group to which he belongs.

8 Before you speak, consider the feelings of the other person. Remember that all human beings have feelings and emotions and that these are important. A hasty, ill-considered word can easily spoil your relationship with another person. If you make such a mistake, make every effort to rectify it as soon as possible.

9 Take every opportunity to make the other person feel important. Everyone likes to feel important and it is often easy to supply such an opportunity.

10 Remember that each person is unique. We cannot expect every person to see things as we do, or feel the same way as we do. Many mistakes in social relations are based on the mistake of trying to treat everybody alike.

Although these principles seem simple, their application requires considerable effort and practice in the everyday situations in which we work, play, and live. They have a solid foundation in psychological fact and if intelligently used will make a great difference to our relations with other people.

Bibliography

The bibliography covers the work of Karl S. Bernhardt from 1934 to 1965. Where an article has been reprinted under the same title in another publication, the reference to the second publication is included with the first. Book entries are preceded by an asterisk (*).

1934 *An Introduction to Psychology. Toronto: Life Underwriters Assoc.
The effect of vitamin B deficiency during nursing on subsequent learning in the rat. J. Comp. Psych., 1934, 17, 123–48.
1935 The selection and guidance of college students. Ont. Voc. Guid. Assoc. Bull., Sept., no. 5.
1936 Who should go to college? Can. School J., 14 (10).
Protein deficiency and learning in rats. J. Comp. Psych., 22, 269–72.
Phosphorus and iron deficiencies and learning in rats. J. Comp. Psych., 22, 273–6.
Vitamin A deficiency and learning in the rat. J. Comp. Psych., 22, 277–8.
1937 Psychology in the selling of life insurance. Canadian Insurance, 42 (30).
A further study of vitamin B deficiency and learning with rats. J. Comp. Psych., 24, 263–7. (With R. Herbert)
The effect of cues on the choice of the shorter path. J. Comp. Psych., 24, 269–76. (With D. Snygg)
An analysis of the social behavior of preschool children with the aid of motion pictures. University of Toronto Child Development Series, no. 10. (With D. A. Millichamp, M. W. Charles, and M. P. McFarland)
1938 The psychology of everyday life. Hardware and Metal, 50, 40–1.
1939 Objectives in parent education. Parent Educ. Bull., no. 5.
1940 What a good home is like. Parent Educ. Bull., no. 9.
Children in a strange land. Parent Educ. Bull., no. 10.
Progressive discipline, the control of the child from birth to maturity. Parent Educ. Bull., no. 11.
Psychology and merchandising in marketing organization. University of Toronto Press, 1940.
Outlines for Parent Education Groups: Discipline. University of Toronto Child Development Series, no. 17. (With W. E. Blatz, D. A. Millichamp, F. L. Johnson, and N. Foster)
1941 Character education. Parent Educ. Bull., no. 12.
Home and school, two institutions with the same goal. Parent Educ. Bull., no. 13.
Parents can solve their own problems. Parent Educ. Bull., no. 14.
Sex education. Parent Educ. Bull., no. 15.
Leisure time activities for the school age child. Parent Educ. Bull., no. 16.
Exploratory studies of abnormal behavior in the rat. J. Comp. Psych., 32, 575–82. (With T. J. Tobin and E. Signori)
1942 Homework, parental worry or opportunity? Parent Educ. Bull., no. 17.
Influences, good and bad. Parent Educ. Bull., no. 20.
The human factor in accidents. Industrial Accident Prevention Assoc., University of Toronto.
A reasonable scheme of discipline. School., 31 (1), 4–8.
*Basic principles of pre-school education. University of Toronto Press. 16 pp.
Christmas and a world at war. The Counsellor, 1942, 13 (2), 1 (reprinted from Parent Educ. Bull.).
1943 Summer activities of the family. Parent Educ. Bull., no. 22.
Growing up in a world at war. Parent Educ. Bull., no. 23.
The first five years. Parent Educ. Bull., no. 24.
The forgotten years, six to twelve. Parent Educ. Bull., no. 25.
*Elementary Psychology. Toronto: Life Underwriters Assoc. 300 pp.

The management of young children. *J. Can. Dental Assoc.*, 9, 209–11 and *Dentistry*, 3, 750–2.

Home and school. *School*, 32, 280–4.

1944   Young adults, or just children. *Parent Educ. Bull.*, no. 26.

Achieving maturity. *Parent Educ. Bull.*, no. 27.

Family life to-day. *Parent Educ. Bull.*, no. 28.

Rewards and punishments in child training. *Parent Educ. Bull.*, no. 29 and *The School*, 1945, 33, 567–70.

Vocational guidance, advantages and dangers. *Parent Educ. Bull.*, no. 30.

Camping for the younger child. *Camping Magazine*, (Feb.), 16(2), 2–3.

The use of rewards and punishments in child training. *Home and School Quart.*, 13(1), 29–32.

Proceedings of the annual meeting of the Can. Psych. Assoc. *Bull. Can. Psych. Assoc.*, 4, 33–4.

The human factor in accident prevention. *Accident Prevention Assoc.*, Nov., 1–8.

1945   Help them grow up. *Parent Educ. Bull.*, no. 31.

Rate your home. *Parent Educ. Bull.*, no. 30.

Healthy parents – healthy children. *Parent Educ. Bull.*, no. 31.

Education for family living. *Parent Educ. Bull.*, no. 32.

Religious education. *Parent Educ. Bull.*, no. 33.

Proceedings of the annual meeting of the Can. Psych. Assoc., *Bull. Can. Psych. Assoc.*, 5.

Practical Psychology. New York: McGraw Hill. 319 pp.

Do you believe in Santa Claus? *Ont. Home and School Review*, 22(2), 13.

Education for safety. *Industrial Accident Prevention Assoc.*, Report of the 1945 Annual Meeting and Convention, 47–54.

Holiday activities in the family. *Ont. Home and School Review*, 22 (Dec.), 29. (Reprinted from *Parent Educ. Bull.*)

1946   The democratic home. *Parent Educ. Bull.*, no. 34.

Summer is the time for play. *Parent Educ. Bull.*, no. 36 and *Our Children*, 1950, 3(3), 2.

Routines for the young child. *Parent Educ. Bull.*, no. 37.

Teenage puzzles. *Parent Educ. Bull.*, no. 37.

Parent child relationships. *Parent Educ. Bull.*, no. 38.

A father writes to his son. Series of short letters in *Parent Educ. Bull.*

The human element in industry. International Assoc. of Printing House Craftsmen. 15 pp.

Happy homes. *Talk*, 27(3), 5.

Human relations in industry. *Can. Paint and Varnish Magazine.*, 20(3), 36.

Report of address. *Can. Printer and Publisher*, 55(6), 64.

Parents can solve their own problems. *Baby News*, 1(1), 6–8.

Routine is a serious business. *Baby News*, 1(2), 19–22.

Making eating a pleasure. *Baby News*, 1(4), 6–7.

Elementary Psychology. Toronto: Life Underwriters Assoc.

1947   Each child needs two parents. *Parent Educ. Bull.*, no. 39.

Are parents a nuisance? *Parent Educ. Bull.*, no. 39.

Tomorrow's citizens. *Parent Educ. Bull.*, no. 40.

Parents can be problems too. *Parent Educ. Bull.*, no. 41.

Getting along with others. *J. of Living*, (Sept.), 21–4. (From *Practical Psychology*)

Psychological methods of personnel selection in industry. *Quart. Rev. Commerce*, 13, 103–7.

Canadian psychology – past, present and future. *Can. J. Psych.*, 1, 49–60. (Canadian Psychological Association, Presidential Address)

Mental hygiene in education. *School Guidance Worker.* 2(5), 1–4.

Psychology of everyday life. *Proceedings, Life Insurance Inst. Can.*, 85–9.

Mental health at home. *Health*, (Nov.), p. 12.

What do I get out of it? *Industrial Accident Prevention Assoc.*, Report of the 1947 annual meeting and convention. 119–26.

1948 Help for confused parents. *Parent Educ. Bull.*, no. 42.

Mental health at work. *Health* (Jan.), 9.

Mental health through play. *Health* (Mar.), 13.

The effect of added thiamine on intelligence and learning with identical twins. *Can. J. Psych.*, 2, 56–61. (With M. L. Northway and C. M. Tatham)

You can build success from failure. *Chatelaine* (June), 24.

Your mental health. *Salesman's Digest* 6(2), 22–4.

Report on developmental and educational psychology. *Can. J. Psych.*, 2, 16–17.

Rx for personal mental health. *Manufacturers Life Newsletter*, 46(3), 3–5 and *Best's Insurance News*, 3, 25–7.

A mental hygiene approach to education. *Can. Ed.*, 3, 7–10.

The parent problem. *Talk* (May), 9.

Confusion and certainties in child study. *Bull. Inst. Child Stud.*, no. 43.

Parents can solve their own problems. *Bull. Inst. Child Stud.*, no. 44.

Families are what we make them. *Bull. Inst. Child Stud.*, no. 45.

Frustrations and what we can do about them. *Can. Credit Inst. Bull.* (Feb.), no. 187.

Human factor in industry. *Can. Purchaser*, 28(10), 64.

A report of an address by KSB. *Ont. Home and School Review*, 12.

1950 Character Education. *Bull. Inst. Child Stud.*, no. 46.

What it means to be a good parent. *Bull. Inst. Child Stud.*, no. 47.

What the child needs – leisure time activities. *British Columbia Parent-Teacher*, 17(11), 4.

Socialization of the child. *Ontario Educ. Assoc. 1950 Year Book*, 22.

1951 A philosophy of discipline. *Bull. Inst. Child Stud.*, no. 48.

Leisure time activities for the school age child. *Bull. Inst. Child Stud.*, 1951, no. 49.

*A prophet not without honour – the contribution of William E. Blatz to child study. Chapter 1 in *Twenty-five years of child study*, Toronto: University of Toronto Press and *Bull. Inst. Child Stud.*, no. 50–1.

Children need discipline. *Can. Homes and Gardens* (Jan.), 46.

Maybe your child is too good. *Can. Homes and Gardens* (Feb.), 35.

If your child is bad. *Can. Homes and Gardens* (Nov.), 22.

Parent education in Canada. *Health* (Jan.-Feb.), 11.

Discipline. *The Junior Leader*, 13(3), 8.

Mental health and the nurse. *The Canadian Nurse*, 47(8), 563.

Motivation in the school age child. *Education*, 72, 263–6.

1952 Character begins at home. *Bull. Inst. Child Stud.*, 1952, 14(3).

Reading for pleasure. *Bull. Inst. Child Stud.*, 1952, 14(4), *Recreation*, 1953, (Nov.), 365 and *Community Courier*, 1953 (Feb.), 1–4.

School Discipline. *Indian School Bull.*, 6(3), 10–11.

*A guide to nursery education. University of Toronto Press. (With M. Fletcher and D. Millichamp)

Happy ever after. *Brides Book* (Fall).

Child study. *Ont. Psych. Assoc. Newsletter*, 5(2), 42–3.

Social relations (report of address). *Marketing* (Nov. 29), 19.

Middle of the road discipline. *Star Weekly*, Mar. 1, 7.

Teenage puzzles. *Can. Home and School*, 12(2), 16–17.

1953 Parent education. *Bull. Inst. Child Stud.*, 1953, 15(1).

The home and school. *Bull. Inst. Child Stud.*, 15(3) and *School Guid. Worker*, 9(3).

Practical Psychology. New York: McGraw Hill (2nd. ed.).

Home and school – cooperating institutions. *Can. Home and School*, 12(3), 8–10.

1954 Sex education. *Bull. Inst. Child Stud.*, 1954, 16(1).

Parent education and mental health. *Bull. Inst. Child Stud.*, 1954, 16(2).

Child development, a foundation for world mental health. *Bull. Inst. Child Stud.*, 1954, 16(4).

Elementary psychology. Toronto: Life Underwriters Assoc. (2nd. ed.).

Mental Health. *Anaconda Spearhead*, 17(2).

Principles of human relationships. *Your Life* (Apr.), 82. (Reprinted from *Practical Psychology*).

1955 Adolescents need understanding. *Bull. Inst. Child Stud.*, 1955, 17(2) and *Health*, 1957 (May-June), 6.

Report of the research symposium on mental health and child development. University of Toronto Press, 11 pp.

Child development. *School guidance worker*, 10(5) Reprinted.

What should we give them? *Health and Physical Educ.* (Oct.-Nov.) (Reprinted from *Bull. Inst. Child Stud.*, 16(3)).

Human relations. *Can. J. Occupational Therapy*, 22, 137–8.

1956 How permissive are you? *Bull. Inst. Child Stud.*, 1956, 18(2).

Laying a foundation for mental health in childhood. *Relig. Educ.*, 51, 328–31.

Is child psychology a fad? *Can. Home J.* (Oct.).

Should you spank your child? *Can. Home J.* (Nov.).

Teach your child Christmas giving. *Can. Home J.* (Dec.).

Making the most of your college career (with D. K. Bernhardt). Toronto: Burns & MacEachern, 59 pp.

1957 The Father in the family. *Bull. Inst. Child Stud.*, 19(2).

Child development in psychology conferences. *Bull. Inst. Child Stud.*, 19(4).

Help for confused parents. *Canadian Welfare*, 32(7), 334–40.

This is my very own. *Nat. Parent-Teacher*, 52(3), 13–15.

Canadian Home Journal series: Jan. – How to spoil your child; Feb. – Meals can be pleasant, even with children; Mar. – Take it easy, mother; Apr. – Should children do chores?; May – War in the nursery; June – How to deal with temper tantrums; July – How to plan family fun; Aug. – The wonderful world of two; Sept. – Children need things of their own; Oct. – How your emotions affect your child; Nov. – Parents and school must work together; Dec. – How do you rate as a parent?

Memo to parents. *Toronto Telegram*, 1–8.

1958 Parental dilemmas, choices and values. *Bull. Inst. Child Stud.*, 20(1).

The "undone" things. *Bull. Inst. Child Stud.*, 20(3).

Building security in a changing world. *Bull. Inst. Child Stud.*, 20(4).

Living with children. Tangley Oaks Educational Center. A series of four child guidance booklets for parents. Twelve articles by Karl S. Bernhardt included.

Canada. *World Topics Year Book*, Tangley Oaks Educational Center.

The role of the parent. *Community Courier*, no. 115, 7–8.

What to tell the child. *Parents Action League*, Toronto.

Canadian Home Journal series: Jan. – The right time and place for t.v.; Feb. – Sex Education is your responsibility; Mar. – Is your child ready to start school?; Apr. – What makes a good home?; May – Adoption, disobedience, stuttering; June – How and when to say "No."

1959 A philosophy of discipline. *Bull. Inst. Child Stud.*, 21(1).

Children's emotions can be respectable. *Bull. Inst. Child Stud.*, 1959, 21(3), *Christian Living*, 1960, 7 (July), 6–7, *Spec. Educ.*, 1960, 34(3), 87–91, and *Blue Print for Health*, 1961 (Fall), 15(4), 10.

A security theory of personality and mental health and samples of relevant research, *Proc. Intern. Congress Psych.*

The parent of to-day can't return to an old pattern. Toronto: *Globe Magazine*, Mar. 14, 10.

The joy of parenthood. *Welfare Reporter*, 18(2), 4.

Ten ways you can beat tensions. *Modern Purchasing*, 1(5), 37.

The child and his anxieties. *New York Post*, Dec. 20, 10.

T. Cook. *Can. Psych.*, 8, 10–11.

Attitude change in members of parent education groups. *Mental Hygiene*, 43, 394–9. (With F. L. Johnson, N. Foster, M. Brown)

1960 Freedom and discipline as a means toward self-discipline. *Bull. Inst. Child Stud.*, 22(3) and *Christian Growth*, 1962, 10(4), 17–23.

How to behave when children misbehave. *Nat. Parent-Teacher*, 1960 54(5), 10–12 and *Growing*, 1962, 15(1), 18.

Mental Health research problems – Canada. *International Mental Health Research Newsletter*, 2, 2.

What you should know about your personality. *Chatelaine* (Aug.), 67.

Spoil the child. *Growing* (Oct.-Dec.), 10–13.

*Your child's world. Lake Bluff, Ill.: Book House for Children (eds.), 160 pp. (With E. E. Sentman)

1961 Dr. Blatz and the Institute. *Bull. Inst. Child Stud.*, 1961, 23(1).

Feeling, affection and happiness in children. *Bull. Inst. Child Stud.*, 1961, 23(2), *Blue-Print for Health*, 1962 (Spring), 16(2), 15, and *Spec. Educ.*, 1962, 36(2), 73–7.

*Training for research in psychology. Toronto: University of Toronto Press.

Toronto's Institute of Child Study, present and future. *Canada's Mental Health* (Feb.), 9 (2), 1–5.

Child development and family living in a home economics programme. *Can. Home Econ. J.*, 11, 9–10 and 29–31.

Publications of Canadian Psychologists 1 – Books. *Can. Psych.*, 2a, 50–2.

Child development and family living in a home economics programme. *Ont. Educ. Assoc. Home Econ. Section Newsletter* (Summer), 6.

1962 Why men work. *Hospital Admin.* (May).

The case for taking children away from their parents. *Macleans*, June 16, 75(12), 18.

A positive, non-punitive scheme of discipline. *Bull. Inst. Child Stud.*, 24(3), 1–10 and *Education*, 1962, 5(5), 29–34.

Education for family life. *Bull. Inst. Child Stud.*, 24(4), 1–11.

1963 It's never too late. *Growing*, 15(3), 12.

Character development in children. *Bull. Inst. Child Stud.*, 25(2), 1–7.

The school and mental health. *Bull. Inst. Child Stud.*, 25(4), 1–4.

Where does character come from? *New York Times Magazine*. (Reprinted from *Bull. Inst. Child Stud.*)

1964 *Discipline and child guidance. New York: McGraw Hill, 322 pp.

1965 Dr. William E. Blatz. *Can. Psych.*, 6a, 1–3.

Editor. *Parent Education Bulletin* and *Bull. Institute of Child Study* from 1938 to 1964.

Index

CANADIAN UNIVERSITY PAPERBOOKS

Titles of related interest in the series